MW00396865

TM.

MISSION 16W

The Colorado Avalanche: 2001 Stanley Cup Champions

MISSION 16W

The Colorado Avalanche: 2000-2001 Stanley Cup Champions

THE DENVER POST   **The SportingNews**

Contents

PHOTO CREDITS

The Denver Post —

Cyrus McCrimmon: 8, 58, 60BL, 61B, 142BL.

Glenn Asakawa: 10, 139TL, 142TL, 143TL.

Hyoung Chang: 11, 15T, 27R, 42, 45B, 60T, 60BR, 61TR, 62, 64B, 68B, 69B, 82R, 87T, 87BL, 87BR, 88, 90BL, 96T, 96B, 97T, 97B, 102T, 102B, 103B, 104B, 105BR, 108, 111B, 115T, 115B, 116T, 120T, 121BL, 121BR, 122T, 122M, 123BL, 127MR, 129BL, 132B, 134B, 137TL, 137TR, 140L, 140TR, 143TR.

John Leyba: 12, 15B, 18BL, 18R, 21T, 26T, 32, 34, 44TL, 44TR, 44B, 45T, 48TR, 49T, 49B, 66, 68T, 69T, 74L, 74TR, 74BR, 75R, 76, 78B, 79T, 90TL, 90R, 91T, 91B, 98, 100, 103T, 104T, 105TR, 109T, 109B, 110, 112, 114, 116B, 120B, 121T, 123T, 123BR, 127T, 127ML, 127B, 128T, 128B, 129TL, 129TR, 129BR, 132T, 133T, 133BL, 133BR, 135BL, 136T, 136BL, 136BR, 138M, 138B, 139TR, 139B, 144T, 144B.

Andy Cross: 18TL, 22R, 24T, 29T, 48L, 48B, 50, 52L, 52TR, 52BR, 53T, 53BL, 53BR, 54, 56T, 56B, 57, 72, 75B, 78T, 79B, 80, 82L, 86L, 86R, 126T.

Brian Brainerd: 20B.

Karl Gehring: 138TL, 138TR.

Craig Walker: 140BR.

Helen Davis: 141TR, 142BR, 143BR, 143TR.

The Sporting News —

Dilip Vishwanat: 2, 16R, 27L, 83TL, 83TR, 83B, 106, 111T, 117T, 117B, 118, 122BR, 124, 126B, 130, 134T, 135T, 135BR, 137B.

Albert Dickson: 14, 16TL, 17T, 17B, 21B, 24B, 26BR, 84.

Bill Sallaz for *The Sporting News:* 94.

Scott Rovak for *The Sporting News:* 16BL.

ALLSPORT —

Brian Bahr: 36, 38.

Jeff Gross: 64L, 64T, 65.

Tim DeFrisco: 2.

Bryan Kelsen/Wide World Photos: 46

T = top, B = bottom, M = middle, R = right, L = left.

Cover—

Front cover: Tim DeFrisco (Ray Bourque). Brian Bahr/ALLSPORT (Joe Sakic). Doug Pensinger/ALL-SPORT (Patrick Roy).

Back cover: Tim DeFrisco.

Copyright © 2001 Vulcan Sports Media, DBA The Sporting News, 10176 Corporate Square Drive, Suite 200, St. Louis, MO 63132. All rights reserved. Printed in the U.S.A.

No part of Mission 16W: The Colorado Avalanche: 2000-2001 Stanley Cup Champions may be reproduced or transmitted in any form or by any means, electronic or mechanical, including photocopy, recording or any other information storage and retrieval system now known or to be invented, without permission in writing from the publisher, except by a reviewer who wishes to quote brief passages in connection with a review written for inclusion in a magazine, newspaper or broadcast.

The Sporting News is a federally registered trademark of Vulcan Sports Media, Inc. Visit our website at www.sportingnews.com.

ISBN: 0-89204-665-1

ACKNOWLEDGEMENTS

The magnitude of this project—to adequately recapture an entire regular-season then game-by-game of the postseason, all in a short amount of time—was exceeded by the willingness and ability of a talented group of people who were very much dedicated to this book.

We must first thank a number of people at *The Denver Post.* Sports Editor Kevin Dale for fielding the initial query to partner on this project; Deputy Sports Editor David Wright for keeping the project moving on a fast track; Assistant Managing Editor Larry Price for providing the images from the preseason to the parade; writers Terry Frei and Adrian Dater for the thousands of words that describe what this season was all about.

At *The Sporting News,* thanks must go to Senior Editor Joe Hoppel, who walked into this project cold one day and committed himself to getting it done; Assistant Editors David Walton and Jeff Paur for their editing assistance; Managing Editor Paul Grant and his cadre of hockey writers, Larry Wigge and Ray Slover, for capturing the Stanley Cup Finals.

Thanks, too, to art director Bob Parajon and designers Michael Behrens, Christen Sager and Matt Kindt, and those who enhanced the digital images in this book, Chris Barnes-Amaro, Dave Brickey and Steve Romer.

Special thanks should also go to the fine photographers at *The Denver Post* and *The Sporting News*—their names accompany the credits for their photos. Their pictures truly recapture the moments of this season.

From all those I've mentioned, and the few I may have inadvertently left off, we hope you enjoy this book as much as we enjoyed putting it together for you.

Steve Meyerhoff
Editorial Director, Books Publishing Division

WHEN THE STANLEY CUP CHAMPION AVS WERE HONORED IN DOWNTOWN DENVER TWO DAYS AFTER GAME 7 OF THE FINALS, FANS WERE EAGER TO SEE JOE SAKIC—AND THE LUSTROUS ITEM HE WAS CARRYING.

Mission Accomplished By Terry Frei

Wearing their white jerseys, the Stanley Cup champions rode on fire trucks down Denver's 17th Street. They waved to fans packed between the storefronts and the street along a 16-block route. Many of the civilian celebrants never had attended an Avalanche game. Yet six seasons into the Avs' stay in Denver, those Coloradans felt attached to the team—as if they were a part of the spirited Pepsi Center crowds.

After the hour-long victory parade on the fire engines, the Avalanche players jumped off the trucks at the Denver City and County Building. A few minutes later, they were introduced one by one, gathering on the steps of the historic building and looking out over the assembled throng of about 250,000 on the grassy Civic Plaza.

Surprisingly, most of them were clean-shaven.

About half of the team had stopped shaving when the postseason began. It was the players' salute—yes, a bit itchy and scratchy—to what Ray Bourque had called "Mission 16W." And there were hats and shirts to commemorate it.

Even Bourque's salt-and-pepper beard was gone. It would live on, though, in the unforgettable pictures of Bourque, all misty-eyed and with a triumphant countenance that had been stored up for 22 seasons, hoisting the Stanley Cup following the Game 7 victory over New Jersey.

Jon Klemm and Greg de Vries, the steady and unheralded defensemen who only 36 hours earlier looked as if they could have been cast in a movie as reclusive fur trappers, didn't even have 5 o'clock stubble.

Shjon Podein, the valuable third-line winger, hadn't found the time to shave. No surprise there. This was a guy who hadn't even taken off his uniform or his skates—yes, his skates—before showing up at the team party at the Denver Chop House following the Cup clincher.

Peter Forsberg, unable to play in the final two playoff series after undergoing an emergency removal of his spleen, saw the sign that gave a new twist to the team's motto: "One Team, One Goal, One Spleen." The Swedish center laughed.

One by one, the stars and role players alike were called out onto a huge stairway, high-fiving as if they had been reunited after months apart.

David Aebischer, the first Swiss-born player to get his name etched on the Stanley Cup, walked out with a camcorder in his palm, so he would have something to show his family back home. That was as much a part of the celebration as Patrick Roy's wave and nod, a nod that didn't live up to the twitching under his mask, but it nonetheless got the message across.

And Joe Sakic waited.

During the speeches and presentations on that Monday afternoon in June, Sakic lingered inside the building—with the Cup.

"We want Joe!" the crowd chanted.

The fans didn't just want the Avalanche captain, though. They wanted what he would carry.

As the Avalanche players and staff looked out, they could see the gleaming Capitol dome beyond the crowd. They could see children with replica jerseys of their favorite players. They could spot the men and women in business attire on long lunch breaks from their offices. They could see signs of congratulations and, in some cases, placards imploring them to re-sign with the Avs.

This was the Colorado's fourth major league championship celebration in five years, and City and County officials had the routine down pat. So did the fans. No longer was there an atmosphere of disbelief, with Coloradans essentially asking: "Is this really happening?"

They were over it by 2001, having experienced the Avalanche's Stanley Cup victory in 1996, then the Denver Broncos' Super Bowl championships in the 1997 and 1998 seasons.

This had a different feel.

It wasn't about giddiness, or—on the other extreme—a market becoming immune to championship excitement. No, it was more about a market that had landed the Quebec Nordiques franchise in 1995 and had to wait a mere nine months for a Stanley Cup championship team—and, in general, not fully appreciating it. That was because Colorado and the Avalanche still were getting to know one another.

In 1996, the Avalanche's honeymoon period—the newness—was multiplied exponentially by the championship run. Colorado came to know and love that team, but the buildup—and the wait for the parade—lasted less than a year.

True passion requires components of perseverance, of relative struggles, even of disappointment. After the Avalanche tantalized and frustrated its fans with three losing trips to the Western Conference finals since the 1996 championship, Colorado had developed that kind of passion for the Avalanche in 2001.

It primarily was a matter of time, not a matter of education.

When the Avalanche arrived, the myth was that Coloradans didn't know hockey, which was laughable, and for a lot of reasons. Many Coloradans come from other places, where they were reared as fans of the Flyers and the Blackhawks and the Rangers and the Bruins and the Red Wings.

Some Coloradans, though, have been hockey fans for decades, following the University of Denver, Colorado College and various professional franchises that included the old Colorado Rockies (who packed up and moved to New Jersey in 1982 and became the Devils).

And, yes, there is the fact—which is absolutely nothing to be ashamed of—that the Avs have turned on many other Coloradans to the sport.

Was Colorado lucky that the team's original Denver owners didn't get what was really wanted—an expansion team that would have begun play when the Pepsi Center opened? Was it lucky that the Nordiques had taken the risk of hiring a longtime player agent, Pierre Lacroix, as general manager a year before the franchise shift? And was it lucky that the team had some of the most promising young talent in the NHL when it was moved to Denver?

Absolutely.

Should Colorado feel a little sympathy for hockey-mad but small-market Quebec City, where the game indeed is a passion—but the passion didn't translate into the construction of the requisite new arena?

You bet.

But after six seasons, this truly is Colorado's team, not a transient.

The franchise hasn't confessed to an unsold ticket since November 1995. And despite a turnover of personnel that meant only six players were on both the 1996 and 2001 championship teams, the Avs have evolved into the No. 2 team in town. They are behind only the Broncos, whose two Super Bowl titles were appreciated all the more by those who had been around long enough to remember the vertically striped socks, hideous uniforms and terrible teams in a time when Denver was viewed in many quarters as less than "major league."

With the Avalanche, it is a bandwagon effect, certainly. Still, there is something to be said for the fans' willingness to put down the money. After all, the deep-rooted Canadian franchises are struggling financially. Thousands of seats go unsold in cities where children can recite the team's top 10 scorers in each of the past 10 seasons.

The Avs now have astounding television ratings.

AVALANCHE
FANS
REVELED
IN THEIR
TEAM'S
ABILITY
TO ACHIEVE
WHAT IT
SET OUT
TO DO.

Hockey has become as much a topic after Sunday Mass at St. Dominic Catholic Church in Denver, near the Pepsi Center, as it is at St. Dominic in coach Bob Hartley's hometown of Hawkesbury, Ont.

Again, it isn't about increased knowledge of the sport, although that's surely part of the increase in popularity for some. Beyond that, it's more about an increased familiarity with the franchise and the assimilation of the franchise into the market. Plus, so many of the young people attending games at the Pepsi Center, or watching Avs telecasts, or standing in the crowd at the Civic Center that Monday, play hockey in one of the busy rinks built since the Avalanche came to town.

Colorado fans are now arguing over whether Ville Nieminen should be on the Peter Forsberg line. They know the stories. They know Sakic's parents emigrated from Croatia to Canada, and that Joe spoke Croatian in his home until he started school. They know that Hartley worked in a windshield factory until he was 27 and got into coaching in his native Hawkesbury virtually by accident. They know that Alex Tanguay, who

scored two goals in Game 7 of the Finals, was drafted with the choice acquired from San Jose for the highly popular Mike Ricci—a trade the fans finally have gotten over. They know of Chris Drury's championship background, at the Little League World Series, at Boston University and with the Avalanche. They know Dan Hinote wanted to be an FBI agent and was a spit-and-polish West Point cadet for two years before leaving to pursue a hockey career.

All right, fans sometimes wonder why the Avs aren't more aggressive in penalty-killing situations, and they debate how the Big Three defensemen should be used. And they're not above booing the power play or grumbling when Roy lets in a soft goal.

All of which means the team and the city and the state have come together.

So when Sakic emerged from the City and County Building for the second time in six seasons, carrying the Stanley Cup through ceremonial smoke, and the cheers cascaded across the Civic Center, it truly was Colorado's championship—much more than it had been in 1996.

One Team, One Goal

By Adrian Dater

It all started in late May of 2000, in the back of a plane again winging its way from Dallas to Denver with a grumpy passenger list. For the second consecutive season, the Colorado Avalanche team was heading home from Texas without a ticket to the Stanley Cup finals, having been eliminated from Cup contention by the Dallas Stars in the Western Conference finals. On both occasions, the Avs skated off the ice to shouts of "Eddie's better" while Stars goalie Ed Belfour was being mobbed by his teammates.

There, in the back of the chartered jet, Ray Bourque and a handful of the Avs' veteran players conceived the mission: This would be a flight the team would NOT take again in 2001. The next time there would be a Game 7 in any playoff series, it would be in front of thousands of fans wearing white Avalanche sweaters, and the Avs would get home from the game in a car, not a plane.

Have a good, restful summer, they told each other, but come ready for work on Day One of training camp. Next season was going to be different. Next season, every game would be played as if it were the seventh game of the Stanley Cup Finals. A victory over Calgary in November might make the difference in getting home-ice advantage throughout the playoffs.

And so the mission was laid out by Bourque, who still hadn't played on a Stanley Cup winner after completing his 21st NHL season. His teammates chose to accept it: The Avs would be *one team, with one goal*. It was Stanley Cup or bust. Such teammates as Patrick Roy, Adam Foote and Joe Sakic pledged they would get Bourque's name on the Cup once and for all. And he would hold it over his head for all the world to see.

And in the end, that's just what happened.

WHEN HIGHLIGHTS OF PATRICK ROY'S RECORD-SETTING

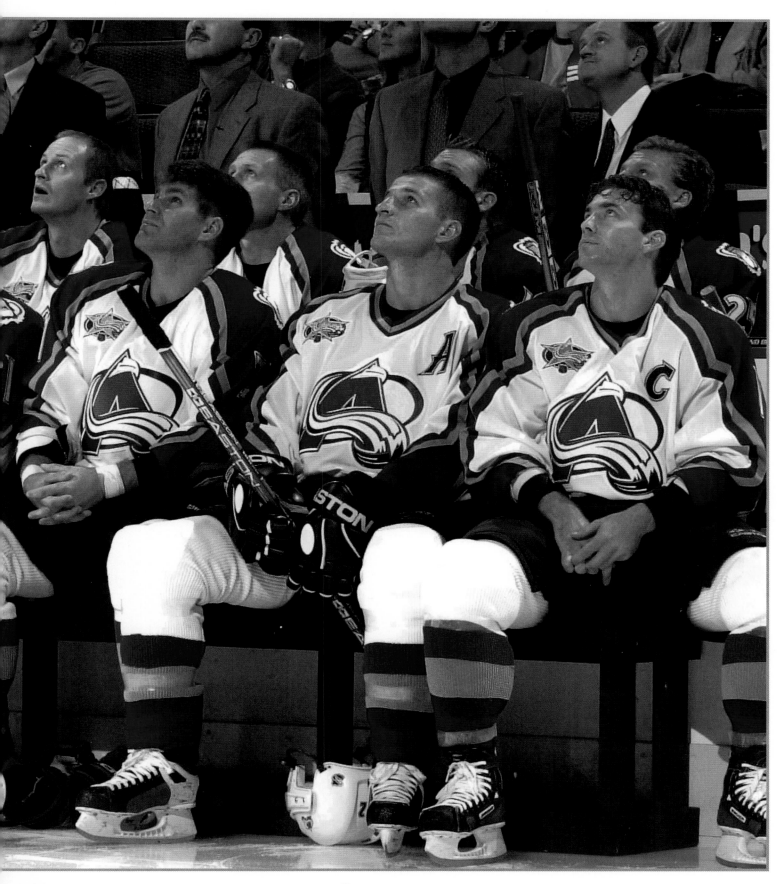

CAREER WERE SHOWN ON A VIDEO BOARD, HIS COLORADO TEAMMATES WATCHED INTENTLY.

The Avalanche accomplished its first item on the season agenda by winning the Presidents' Trophy for best regular-season record (118 points), which guaranteed that no Game 7 would be played anywhere but in Denver's Pepsi Center.

Then, when the playoffs started, Bourque donned a black baseball cap with the words "Mission 16W" on the front. Sixteen wins, and the Cup would belong to Colorado. Even when major adversity struck in the playoffs—superstar center Peter Forsberg was sidelined after the second round because of surgery to remove his spleen—Bourque never put the hat in the closet. He kept in on his head, to remind his teammates that no one player was bigger than the sum of the team's parts.

In the end, he was right. The Avs made it fashionable again for coaches to trot out the cliche, "There is no 'i' in t-e-a-m." In today's megabucks sports world, individuals like Alex Rodriguez sell tickets. But the Avs proved that teams still win championships.

When reflecting on the Avalanche's regular season, it seemed like a breeze. And, relatively speaking, it was. There were few crises, either from injuries or drastic slumps.

The season started in the same place the previous one ended, at Reunion Arena in Dallas, and the Avs quickly fell behind, 2-0, to the two-time Western Conference champion Stars. But a harbinger of how the season would go occurred that night. The Avs didn't win, but they rallied to salvage a tie. Colorado also would tie the second game of the season three nights later against the Edmonton Oilers.

But then the Avs reeled off nine straight victories, and they would relinquish control of the league's best record only for a few days at midseason. One of those nine triumphs came at the MCI Center in Washington, D.C., on October 17. After Forsberg tipped a Bourque

On the way to winning the NHL's Presidents' Trophy for best regular-season record, the Avs got good work from Ray Bourque, Adam Foote (above) and Steven Reinprecht (immediate left).

Among those playing key roles for the
2000-01 Avs were Joe Sakic (No. 19),
Shjon Podein (25), Chris Drury (37),
Jon Klemm (24) and Martin Skoula (41).

shot past Capitals goalie Olaf Kolzig in overtime, Patrick Roy was hoisted onto the broad shoulders of Bourque and Foote and paraded around the ice. It wasn't just any win that night; it was Roy's 448th career victory in goal, which moved him ahead of Terry Sawchuk for No. 1 on the all-time NHL list.

Afterward, in a crowded locker room, Roy took a phone call from Canadian Prime Minister Jean Chretien, who reminded him that he was still a hero in Quebec, even though he had been traded by the Montreal Canadiens to the Avalanche in December 1995.

Winning Stanley Cups has always been Roy's top priority, but Sawchuk's record was one individual honor he very much wanted.

"To me, I think it shows I've been consistent for a long time," Roy said. "I think if you ask any athlete, that means a lot, that they were able to win for a long time. Not just one or two years, but one or two decades."

The season would roll along, with the Avs only once losing more than two games in a row. There were some early-season injury problems, though. Chris Drury, the team's bulldog-like forward with a big heart, was lost for a month after having his knee injured by a hit from the Canucks' Matt Cooke. And, right winger Adam Deadmarsh was sidelined six weeks after being decked in a fight with Vancouver defenseman Ed Jovanovski. Deadmarsh had always been a willing fighter—often to the Avs' dismay. He was a top-six forward whose offense they hated to lose.

Not to worry. As was proved from the opening of the season to the Cup Finals, the Avs simply inserted a new part whenever something broke down in their machine-like team. When Deadmarsh was inactive, it provided an opportunity for happy-go-lucky Ville Nieminen to

Patrick Roy acknowledged the crowd after
it give him a thunderous ovation for breaking Terry Sawchuk's wins record for goalies.
All eyes focused on a bronze statue of Roy.

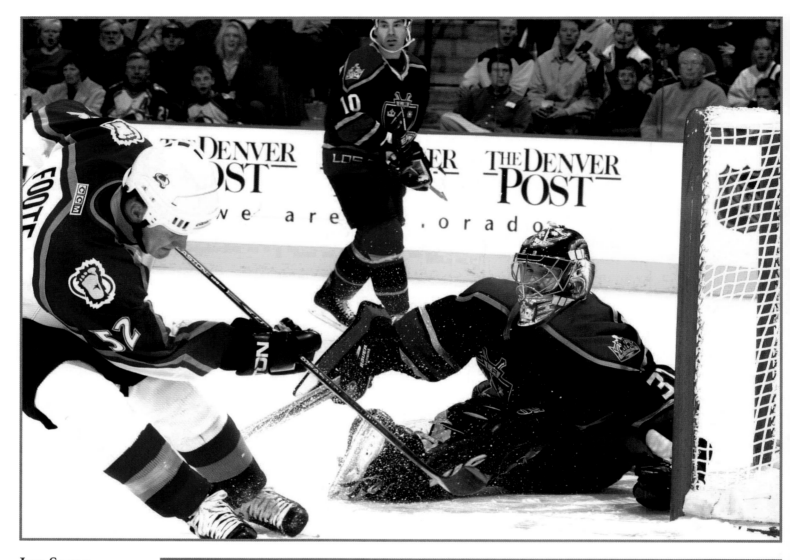

JOE SAKIC (IMMEDIATE RIGHT AND TOP, RIGHT) VOWED TO HAVE A BIG SEASON—AND HE DID. VILLE NIEMINEN (FAR RIGHT) SYMBOLIZED THE AVS' APPROACH TO THE GAME, AND ADAM FOOTE WAS A FORCE.

show his stuff. Nieminen, an abrasive left winger whose style and demeanor are similar to that of Detroit's Tomas Holmstrom, had spent considerable time with the Avs' minor league affiliate in Hershey, Pa. When he was called up to fill in for Deadmarsh, Avalanche fans had never heard of him. Most of his teammates had barely heard of him.

But Nieminen would come to symbolize the Avs' approach to the game. He was tireless, boundlessly enthusiastic and resilient. He scored two goals and added an assist in his first four games after the call-up, and later he would make it easier for Pierre Lacroix, Avalanche team president and general manager, to make a blockbuster trade involving Deadmarsh.

The Avs continued to mow down the opposition on their way to the best regular-season record in franchise history—and Sakic made a mighty contribution. After scoring just two goals in his first 13 games, he went on a tear that would continue through the playoffs.

Sakic, who had notched a career-high 51 goals and 120 points in 1995-96, had been frustrated by injuries from 1996-97 through 1999-2000, missing 66 games in those four seasons. After coming one short of the play-off record for goals with 18 in 22 games in the Avs' first Stanley Cup-winning season, Sakic managed just 18 in his next 59 postseason contests. In the 2000 playoffs, the low-key Avs captain scored just two goals in 17 games, and he took much of the blame for the team's exit.

Among those who vowed in May 2000 that "next year" would be different, no one was more serious about the quest than Sakic. Always religious about his punishing offseason workouts, Sakic rededicated himself even more to the training room, vowing to stay healthy for the first time since playing all 82 games in 1995-96. Sakic would do just that, and his season paralleled not only his '95-96 performance, but mirrored the team's fortunes as well. Sakic played in all 82 regular-season games in 2000-01 and established a career high with 54 goals, including a league-leading 12 game-winners.

Sakic was terrific offensively, centering a unit (Milan Hejduk and Alex Tanguay were his linemates) that terrorized goalies all season. He also finished plus-45 in a season that would earn him the NHL's most valuable player award.

The big trade unfolded on the night of February 21, and it hit the Avalanche dressing room like a

GREG DE VRIES (ABOVE) WAS A STEADY DEFENSEMAN FOR THE AVALANCHE, WHICH GOT ANOTHER STANDOUT SEASON FROM GOALTENDER PATRICK ROY (2.21 GOALS-AGAINST AVERAGE).

thunderbolt. The Avs had just skated to their most lop-sided victory of the season, an 8-2 win over the Boston Bruins.

Deadmarsh had scored two of the Colorado goals against Boston, and there was a festive mood when the final horn sounded at the Pepsi Center that night. Not only did the Avs beat Bourque's longtime team (which meant a big team party, paid for by Bourque, as is the NHL custom when a player beats his old team for the first time), but Colorado was cruising along with the league's best record. Why mess with success? Because, as anyone who has been around Lacroix for long knows, the G.M. realized the present wasn't what mattered the most. He was thinking ahead—to May and June.

And Lacroix knew the old saying "defense wins championships" was almost always true. He was aware that he had a fast, high-scoring team that was exciting to watch. But he also knew that he and his team had failed to win a Stanley Cup in the previous four years. He knew his team had been eliminated by Dallas the past two years because, when playoff time came around and the ice seems to shrink a little, his team had trouble skating against a Stars defense that featured three big-name players on the blue line.

The Avs had a pair of defensive studs in Bourque and Foote. But when Lacroix found out that the Los Angeles Kings had decided to put Rob Blake, a 6-4, 225-pound, former Norris Trophy winner, on the trading block, the Monty Hall instinct in him could not be contained.

Lacroix once said he had a hard time driving by houses with "For Sale" signs in the yard without wanting to knock on the door and make an offer. So the sight of Blake on the auction block was too much for him to resist.

"When you have a chance to get a Rob Blake,"

RAY BOURQUE WAS A FAVORITE WITH DENVER FANS, WHO ALSO APPRECIATED THE 41-GOAL OUTPUT OF MILAN HEJDUK (ABOVE) AND THE PLAY OF ALEX TANGUAY (RIGHT), WHO CAPPED A BIG SEASON WITH TWO GOALS IN GAME 7 OF THE STANLEY CUP FINALS.

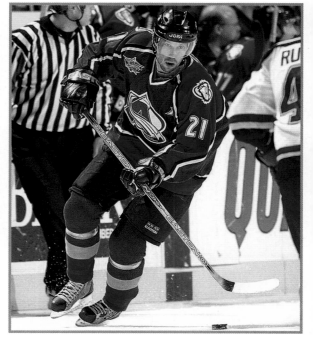

COACH BOB HARTLEY (OPPOSITE PAGE, RIGHT) ENJOYED A BIG
GAIN (ROB BLAKE, OPPOSITE PAGE, LEFT) LATE IN THE SEASON
BUT ENDURED A BIG LOSS (PETER FORSBERG, ABOVE) MIDWAY
THROUGH THE PLAYOFFS.

Lacroix said, "you can't miss."

It didn't matter to Lacroix that Blake could become an unrestricted free agent after the season. So Lacroix pulled the trigger, dealing Deadmarsh, defenseman Aaron Miller and three other high-round draft choices for Blake and Steve Reinprecht. The trade jolted the Avs. Deadmarsh was a highly popular player with his teammates and the fans, and his wife had just delivered twin girls after a difficult pregnancy. Yes, the team had the best record in hockey, but Lacroix clearly was sending a message: The Avs needed to be even better to win it all.

"This is the closest team I've ever played on," one shocked Avs player said after the trade was announced. "To see 'Deader' go like that, with his family situation and all, that's tough."

Some of Lacroix's G.M. brethren criticized the trade. Detroit G.M. Ken Holland said Lacroix paid "a very steep price," and Red Wings center Steve Yzerman said the Avs would miss Deadmarsh. "He's scored a lot of big goals on us," Yzerman said.

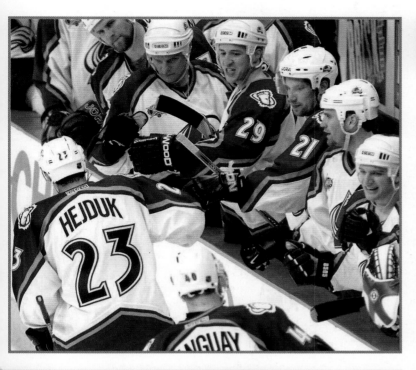

Deadmarsh would do so again as a Kings player, knocking the Red Wings out of the playoffs with a Game-6 overtime goal in the first round. But Lacroix would get the last laugh on Holland and every other general manager who missed out on Blake.

As the end of the regular season drew near, the Avs were pointing toward the playoffs—and a late-March game in Boston. For the first time in 22 NHL seasons, Bourque would play on Boston ice with a sweater that did not have the familiar spoked "B" on the front. In an emotional game, Bourque recorded two assists in a 4-2 Colorado victory. He saluted the sellout Boston crowd, which never got to see him win a Stanley Cup in a Bruins uniform.

But 2½ months later, via television, Boston fans would get to see Bourque lift the Cup over his head in the bedlam that was the Pepsi Center.

On June 9, 2001, some 2,000 miles from Boston and a long time removed from the moment a special concept was conceived in the back of a Dallas-to-Denver airplane, Mission 16W was completed.

WHEN JOE SAKIC ACCEPTED THE PRESIDENTS' TROPHY, IT PROVED THE AVS WERE WELL ON THE WAY TO REALIZING THEIR "ONE TEAM, ONE GOAL" OBJECTIVE—A TOGETHERNESS THAT WAS EVIDENT EVEN ON THE BENCH.

ROUND

1

1W

2W

3W

4W

GAME 1

April 12 at Colorado

Avalanche	5
Canucks	4

The Quebec Nordiques selected a Boston University-bound kid from Connecticut in the third round of the 1994 draft, then settled in for the wait. Two years later, after the franchise had moved to Colorado, coach Marc Crawford of the Nordiques-turned-Avalanche met with the college student, Chris Drury, at the Olympic Festival in Denver. He was impressed.

Crawford never got to coach the young man, though. And when Drury scored twice as the Avalanche beat Vancouver, 5-4, in a 2001 NHL playoff opener at Denver's Pepsi Center, it surely wasn't any consolation for Crawford—now coach of the Canucks—that he was right about the New England youth's potential.

Drury's second goal broke a 4-4 tie with only 67 seconds remaining in regulation. Drury took a pass from Rob Blake, broke in on Vancouver goalie Dan Cloutier, faked him out of position and easily scored on a backhander.

"We didn't want it to go to OT. The way they kept bouncing back, we wanted to end it," Drury said. "Rob just laid it out there in a perfect place for me to go and get it."

The Avs, playing without veteran Ray Bourque (sidelined because of a back injury), also got two goals from Joe Sakic and a goal and three assists from Blake. And Colorado went 3-for-5 on power-play opportunities. All of which helped to offset a rare off night by goalie Patrick Roy.

Jon Klemm (far right) and Shjon Podein were the

FIRST TO CONGRATULATE CHRIS DRURY (MIDDLE, RIGHT) ON HIS LATE GOAL. ROB BLAKE WASN'T FAR BEHIND.

CANUCKS GOALIE BOB ESSENSA HELD OFF THE AVALANCHE FOR TWO PERIODS, BUT HE YIELDED TWO GOALS EARLY IN THE THIRD PERIOD—THIS ONE THE GAME-WINNER OFF THE STICK OF MILAN HEJDUK, WHOSE SHOT CAME ON A 2-ON-1 BREAK WITH JOE SAKIC (RIGHT).

GAME 2

April 14 at Colorado

| Avalanche | 2 |
| Canucks | 1 |

The Canucks switched goalies for Game 2, going with journeyman Bob Essensa, and he responded with a superlative game—for two periods.

Then the Avalanche awakened, getting early third-period goals from Ville Nieminen and Milan Hejduk only 42 seconds apart. The Avs won, 2-1, and seized a two games-to-none lead in the series, which now would shift to Vancouver.

Patrick Roy faced only 19 shots, giving up a second-period, power-play goal to Brendan Morrison, and the Avs again won without Ray Bourque, whose return to action was imminent.

"That was a tough game," said Hejduk, who hadn't scored in the Avs' final seven regular-season games and the playoff opener. "Maybe we thought these first two games would be a little easier or something, but they have not been."

Nieminen pulled the Avs into a 1-1 tie with a soft goal at 2:22 of the third, taking a pass from Peter Forsberg in the right circle and getting off a stoppable shot that Essensa simply mishandled. The puck trickled through his pads and across the line. "I was just trying to get a shot on net," Nieminen said of his first career playoff goal.

Hejduk's game-winner was considerably more artful. On a 2-on-1 break with Joe Sakic, Hejduk took the pass and faked a shot, getting defenseman Murray Baron out of position. Then he drew the puck back and beat Essensa.

PETER FORSBERG WAS BURIED IN AN AVALANCHE OF HAPPY PLAYERS AFTER HIS OVERTIME GOAL STAKED

GAME 3

April 16 at Vancouver

| Avalanche | 4 | (OT) |
| Canucks | 3 | |

Vancouver fans booed the "Star-Spangled Banner" before the game, then littered the ice with trash after Peter Forsberg scored at 2:50 of overtime to give the Avalanche a 4-3 victory and a seemingly insurmountable 3-0 edge in the best-of-seven series.

Forsberg scored the game-winner after the Canucks' Todd Bertuzzi took an ill-advised crosschecking penalty that wiped out a power-play opportunity for the Vancouver club.

Colorado's Steve Reinprecht was headed off for tripping when Bertuzzi crosschecked Colorado's Eric Messier to the back of the head as Messier was down on the ice.

Forsberg's goal came only 43 seconds after Reinprecht and Bertuzzi went off. He cut around defenseman Murray Baron, then lifted a forehand shot over a sprawled Bob Essensa.

"They got a little mixed up, because I was kind of by myself," said Forsberg, who was coming off a 27-goal season. "I just went to the net, and the goalie went down. I just shot it upstairs."

Joe Sakic, Chris Drury and Adam Foote had earlier goals for Colorado, and it was Foote's power-play score that produced a 3-3 tie at 9:52 of the third period.

Ray Bourque was back in the Colorado lineup. He played most of the game in even-strength situations with Foote. Though Bourque appeared a bit rusty at times, his mere presence proved a boost for the Avalanche.

THE GAME WAS SCORELESS LATE IN THE SECOND PERIOD WHEN THE AVS' CHRIS DRURY SLIPPED THE PUCK

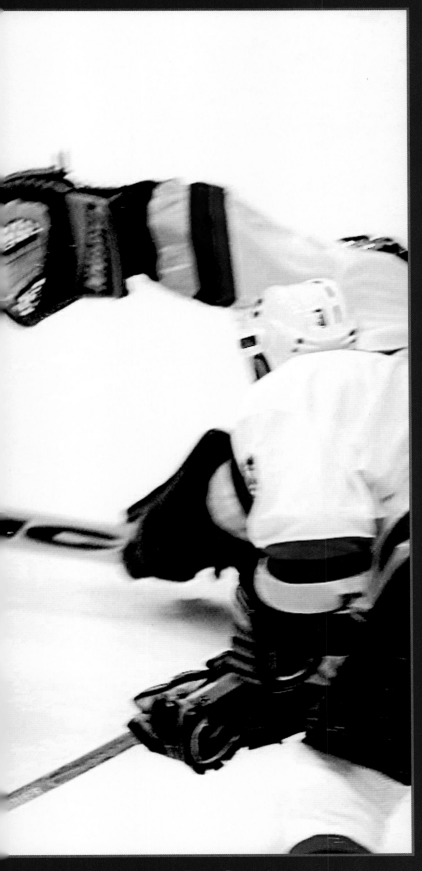

PAST CANUCKS GOALIE DAN CLOUTIER.

GAME 4

April 18 at Vancouver

Avalanche	5
Canucks	I

A 5-1 triumph sounds like a romp, right? Yet the clinching game in Colorado's first-round sweep of Vancouver was a scoreless affair late in the second period when Chris Drury broke through for a power-play goal. The Avs then scored three times in a span of 38 seconds in the third period to put it away.

The Canucks got only 11 shots in the first two periods against Patrick Roy. Dan Cloutier, back in the net for Vancouver because of Bob Essensa's knee injury, was terrific in keeping the Canucks in the game until the Avs' third-period explosion. Until then, the Avalanche had never built a two-goal lead in the series.

Another silly penalty by the Canucks opened the door for Drury's ice-breaking goal. Drake Berehowsky crosschecked Peter Forsberg after the whistle, and Drury then scored as the penalty clock wound down.

"It just kind of opened up," said Drury. "It shows we have some talented guys out there. If we do the right things in our own zone and play sound hockey, any minute we can explode like we did tonight."

Forsberg, Joe Sakic and Eric Messier scored in the third-period siege, and Alex Tanguay's empty-net goal finished it off.

Roy stopped 22 of 23 shots, allowing only a third-period power-play goal to Trent Klatt.

"If you give them a little room to breathe, they will be all over you," Cloutier said. "They have some world-class players, some All-Stars and even a couple of future Hall of Famers."

ROUND
2

5W

6W

7W

8W

PATRICK ROY'S NIGHT ENDED ABRUPTLY WHEN JAROSLAV MODRY WHISTLED A SLAP SHOT PAST HIM. THE KINGS

ADAM DEADMARSH (28) WAS CLOSE TO THE ACTION.

GAME 1

April 26' at Colorado

Kings	4	(OT)
Avalanche	3	

T he Los Angeles Kings, fresh from a stunning comeback in their opening-round conquest of the Detroit Red Wings, maintained their momentum in the second-round opener against the Avalanche.

Colorado was coming off an eight-day layoff, and it showed. Patrick Roy had one of his shakiest postseason games in a storied career, giving up three goals on 16 shots in regulation and then allowing Jaroslav Modry's game-winner on a slap shot from the top of the right circle at 14:23 of overtime. Modry's goal came on a power play—Colorado's Adam Foote had been called for holding—and gave Los Angeles a 4-3 win.

Felix Potvin, a late-season pickup by the Kings, had 34 saves and repeatedly frustrated the Avs. Meanwhile, Roy's reputation as one of the greatest money goalies of all time suddenly was in jeopardy of being sullied.

"I know that when the puck goes through your legs, it never looks good," Roy said. "But I was more upset with their second goal (by Nelson Emerson). The third goal (Glen Murray's) went right over my stick. I thought I was in the right position, and it surprised me a bit."

The Avs forced overtime when Peter Forsberg scored on a third-period power play to tie the game at 3-3. Chris Drury and Rob Blake had the Avs' other goals.

Considering the teams had made a major trade in February—Blake going to Colorado in a deal that sent Adam Deadmarsh to Los Angeles—the series figured to be emotional and fiercely competitive. And after one game, it was proving to be just that.

GAME 1

Ray Bourque was ecstatic (top, middle photo) when Rob Blake scored. Still, Kings goalie Felix Potvin (above) frustrated the Avs despite the efforts of such Colorado players as Ville Nieminen (No. 39) and Chris Drury.

THE GOAL BY BLAKE (LEFT, SKATING OFF THE ICE) GAVE THE AVS THE LEAD IN THE SECOND PERIOD, BUT LOS ANGELES WAS DOING THE CELEBRATING AT GAME'S END (BELOW).

GAME 2

April 28 at Colorado

Avalanche   2
Kings   0

R ay Bourque's swat took only a fraction of a second. But it might have changed the course of the Avalanche's postseason.

Game 2 was scoreless in the second period when one of the strangest sequences in Avalanche playoff history unfolded. Glen Murray's shot caromed off goalie Patrick Roy's shoulder and seemed headed for the net—the Kings thought it crossed the goal line—when Bourque took a baseball swing at the puck and batted it away.

The Kings screamed that it was a goal, but play continued and Colorado's Ville Nieminen knocked a rebound of a Peter Forsberg shot past Felix Potvin at the other end. That came at 2:29 of the second period. Referees Paul Devorski and Don Koharski immediately went upstairs to check the video on Murray's shot. A ruling in favor of Los Angeles would have given the Kings a 1-0 lead and negated Nieminen's goal.

None of the camera angles indicated the puck had crossed the goal line, though, so Murray's shot was ruled "no goal."

If the goal had been allowed, the Kings would have had momentum. But Bourque's play and the swing in fortunes that followed energized the Avs.

Joe Sakic's goal at 15:13 of the third period made it 2-0, and Roy went on to a 20-save shutout. It was the record 16th playoff shutout for the veteran, who appeared back in his postseason groove.

"There's good pressure and bad pressure, and I was putting too much bad pressure on myself," Roy said.

RAY BOURQUE'S SWAT CHANGED THE TRAJECTORY OF A

CAROM—AND MIGHT HAVE CHANGED THE COURSE OF THE AVS-KINGS SERIES, TOO.

MISSION 16W   47   ROUND 2, GAME 2

GAME 2

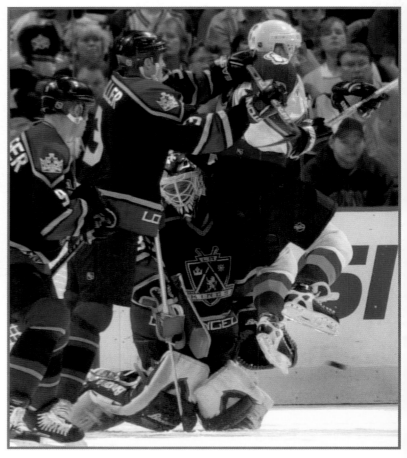

THE AVALANCHE-KINGS PLAYOFF SERIES FEATURED PHYSICAL PLAY—AS COLORADO'S PETER FORSBERG (ABOVE) AND VILLE NIEMINEN (IMMEDIATE RIGHT) COULD ATTEST.

COLORADO GOT GOALS FROM VILLE NIEMINEN (TOP, LEFT) AND JOE SAKIC (LEFT) IN SUPPORT OF PATRICK ROY (ABOVE, WITH ROB BLAKE), WHO NOTCHED THE 16TH PLAYOFF SHUTOUT OF HIS CAREER.

GAME 3

April 30 at Los Angeles

| Avalanche | 4 |
| Kings | 3 |

E very time Colorado defenseman Rob Blake touched the puck, he was booed. It wasn't good-natured, either.

Blake, making his first appearance in Los Angeles since he was dealt by the Kings to Colorado two months earlier, didn't seem to mind the catcalls. After all, he scored the Avalanche's first goal on a 65-foot slap shot at 4:33 of the first period. The way Felix Potvin fouled up that one, it would have been understandable if Los Angeles fans had redirected their invective toward the Kings' goalie. Yet the booing of Blake continued, with Blake's wife and other family members watching the game from the private box that Blake still leases at the Staples Center.

The Avs could deal with the jeers—but not with the possibility of an extended loss of captain Joe Sakic, who left the game after suffering a shoulder injury in the first 5 minutes. Sakic had been crunched in a sandwich hit, taking the brunt of the contact along the boards from Jozef Stumpel and Jere Karalahti.

"It's tender, it's sore and it's day-to-day," Sakic said of his injury.

The Avs nonetheless managed to take a 2-1 lead in the series. Peter Forsberg and Milan Hejduk added goals before Jon Klemm made it 4-2, Avs, with 10:33 left in the third period.

The Kings bombarded Patrick Roy, but the Colorado goalie turned in one of his best games of the postseason despite yielding three goals. One big stop came on a 5-on-3 power play, another on a conventional Kings

IN ROB BLAKE'S FIRST GAME BACK IN LOS ANGELES AFTER

LATE-SEASON TRADE, HE UNLEASHED A 65-FOOT SLAP SHOT THAT BEAT FELIX POTVIN.

GAME 3

power play and the third after the Kings pulled Potvin for a sixth attacker.

Los Angeles was still mounting significant pressure near game's end, and Roy made a big kick save of a Ziggy Palffy redirection to preserve a 4-3 victory.

"Patty was huge for us," Blake said. "It was a tough win. Their crowd was really into it, and they came hard after us. But we stood up to it and got the win."

AN INJURY TO JOE SAKIC (RIGHT, MIDDLE) WAS A BIG CONCERN TO THE AVS, WHO GOT GOALS FROM PETER FORSBERG (FAR RIGHT), MILAN HEJDUK (TOP, LEFT) AND THE GAME-WINNER FROM JON KLEMM (TOP, RIGHT) IN GAME 3. GOALIE PATRICK ROY (ABOVE) CAME UP BIG AS COLORADO SEIZED THE SERIES LEAD IN A ROUGH-AND-TUMBLE GAME IN WHICH ALEX TANGUAY (IMMEDIATE RIGHT) ALSO WAS IN THE MIDDLE OF THE ACTION.

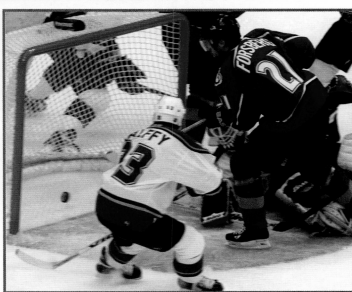

GAME 4

May 2 at Los Angeles

Avalanche   3
Kings   0

This game confirmed one thing: Patrick Roy was back.

The Kings managed only 21 shots—but 10 of them came in a scoreless first period during which Colorado was thoroughly outplayed.

"Unbelievable is the only word," Colorado coach Bob Hartley said of Roy's performance in a 3-0 Avalanche victory. "If it weren't for Patrick, we could have headed back to the hotel after the first period."

Alex Tanguay and Chris Drury each had a goal and an assist, and the Avs took a 3-1 series lead with Joe Sakic watching in street clothes as he rested his injured shoulder. Sakic participated in the morning skate and the pregame warmup, but he was a late scratch.

Milan Hejduk had the Avs' other goal in a game that showcased the Avs' young stars up front. Hartley moved Peter Forsberg into Sakic's spot, centering Hejduk and Tanguay, and he slid Chris Drury over to center on the second line.

"That's the kind of team we have," Roy said after racking up the 17th playoff shutout of his career. "During the season, when we've had adversity, we've always found a way to get the job done."

As the Avs opened a two-game edge in the series, there was no letup in the anti-Blake sentiment expressed by Los Angeles fans—despite speculation that Blake might re-sign with Los Angeles in the offseason. But the booing and Blake's continuing critical remarks about the Kings ownership and management seemed to make the divorce final.

Avs coach Bob Hartley said there was only one word to describe Patrick Roy's performance in Game 4: *UNBELIEVABLE.* Roy fended off 10 Kings shots in the first period en route to another playoff shutout.

GAME 4

2001 Stanley Cup Playoffs
WESTERN CONFERENCE SEMIFINALS

ADAM FOOTE (52), ALEX TANGUAY (40) AND JON KLEMM (24) WHOOP IT UP AFTER TANGUAY'S SECOND-PERIOD GOAL (RIGHT). FOOTE (BELOW, WITH RAY BOURQUE) AND PETER FORSBERG WERE AIRBORNE AT TIMES IN THE FIERCELY CONTESTED GAME.

LOS ANGELES' LUC ROBITAILLE AND ADAM DEADMARSH WERE EUPHORIC AFTER ROBITAILLE SCORED THE ONLY GOAL OF GAME 5. ON THE BRINK OF ELIMINATION, THE RESILIENT KINGS CAME AWAY WITH A STUNNING VICTORY ON COLORADO'S HOME ICE.

GAME 5

May 4 at Colorado

| Kings | 1 |
| Avalanche | 0 |

T his was the beginning of a two-game spell of offensive ineptitude for the Avs, who suddenly looked as if they couldn't put the puck in the Pacific Ocean from the end of the Santa Monica Pier.

It didn't help that Joe Sakic sat out again because of his banged-up shoulder. The prevailing view was that the Avalanche hoped to get by without him while clinching this series, then give Sakic and his shoulder more rest before the Western Conference finals.

The Kings avoided elimination, thanks to Luc Robitaille and Felix Potvin. Robitaille got the only goal of Game 5 at 10:05 of the third period, and the Avs managed only 20 shots against a seemingly impenetrable Potvin.

"There probably weren't a lot of people here in this building (Denver's Pepsi Center) that felt we'd be going back to Los Angeles," Kings coach Andy Murray said. "The busiest guy in the building tonight was the Avalanche travel agent."

The Avs went a puzzling 0-for-6 on the power play in this game, making them 3-for-29 in the series. With Rob Blake and Ray Bourque in the lineup, a devastating power play seemed a given for Colorado.

The Avs thought they had taken a 1-0 lead midway through the second period when Milan Hejduk's whack at a rebound got past Potvin, but a video review waved off the goal. The issue was whether Hejduk's stick had been too high when he hit the puck.

After the game, Colorado coach Bob Hartley refused

GAME 5

to complain, saying the goal should not have been allowed.

"I don't know if we came out flat," said Avalanche center Peter Forsberg, who had three shots on Potvin. "I think we just played stupid."

Whatever the reason for the Avalanche's poor performance, it was becoming clear that Hartley had lost some confidence in second-year defenseman Martin Skoula. The Avs went with five defensemen for most of Game 5, with Skoula taking only spot shifts.

RAY BOURQUE (BELOW, LEFT), PETER FORSBERG (BELOW, RIGHT) AND SHJON PODEIN WERE ON COLLISION COURSES WITH THE OPPOSITION.

KINGS GOALIE FELIX POTVIN AND DEFENSEMAN ANDREAS LILJA (LEFT) TEAMED UP TO THWART CHRIS DINGMAN'S THIRD-PERIOD SCORING ATTEMPT. THE AVS' PATRICK ROY (BELOW) WAS EVER-VIGILANT, TOO.

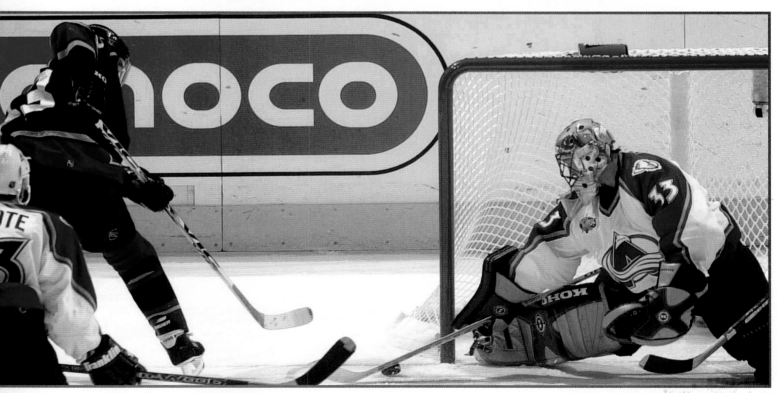

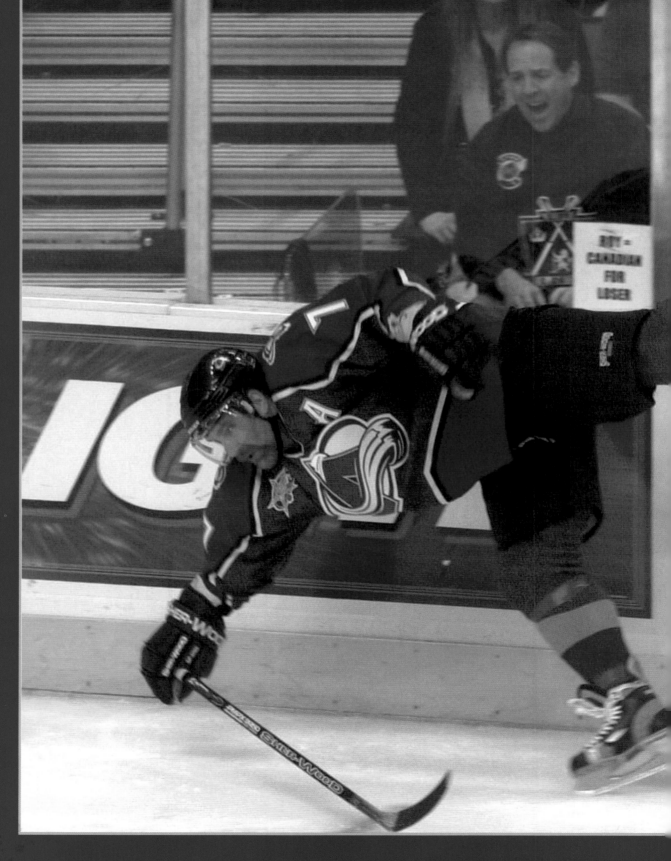

RAY BOURQUE WAS SENT SPRAWLING AFTER BEING CHECKED BY ADAM DEADMARSH. BY GAME'S END, THE AVS—NOW IN A 3-3 SERIES TIE—WERE IN DANGER OF TAKING A COLLECTIVE PRATFALL.

GAME 6

May 6 at Los Angeles

Kings   1
Avalanche   0   (2 OT)

Joe Sakic returned to the lineup, but he was still hurting and didn't take faceoffs. Sakic did manage five of Colorado's 33 shots against Kings goalie Felix Potvin, yet he—and his teammates—couldn't get one past Potvin.

And when Glen Murray's shot from outside the right circle trickled off Patrick Roy and into the net, Game 6 finally ended at 2:41 of the second overtime.

"Seeing it go over the line, it was like, 'Wow, we're going to Game 7,'" said Murray after the Kings' 1-0 victory. "Now it's do or die for both teams."

The Avs suddenly appeared to be in serious trouble. The major concern wasn't that the Kings had sent the series to a seventh game in Denver, but that the Avs' offense—held scoreless for the second consecutive game—was in a terrible slump.

The Avs had a power-play chance in the final minute of regulation, when the Kings inexplicably were caught with too many men on the ice. During the power play, Ray Bourque hauled down Ziggy Palffy to prevent what Bourque thought would be a shorthanded break for the Kings. The man advantage negated, the Avs remained in their scoring funk.

With the series headed back to the Pepsi Center for Game 7, it was obvious that the Kings—with their first-round playoff comeback against Detroit and their showing against Colorado in this series—had rejuvenated NHL interest in the nation's No. 2 market. After the game ended, many Los Angeles fans remained in their seats and chanted, "LET'S GO KINGS!"

GAME 6

LOS ANGELES' GLEN MURRAY (ABOVE) SKATES
TOWARD HIS HAPPY TEAMMATES AFTER ENDING A
LONG NIGHT OF HOCKEY—A VERY LONG NIGHT
FOR THE AVALANCHE—WITH A GOAL AT 2:41 OF
THE SECOND OVERTIME. THE KINGS' FELIX POTVIN
(FAR RIGHT, MAKING A STICK SAVE) AND THE AVS'
PATRICK ROY (TOP, MIDDLE, MAKING A SAVE ON
JOZEF STUMPEL) GAVE A CLINIC ON GOALTENDING
IN THE 1-0 GAME, WHICH FEATURED SOME ROUGH-
AND-TUMBLE PLAY (RIGHT).

RAY BOURQUE SKATED UP TO ROB BLAKE TO CONGRATULATE BLAKE ON HIS FIRST-PERIOD GOAL IN WINNER-

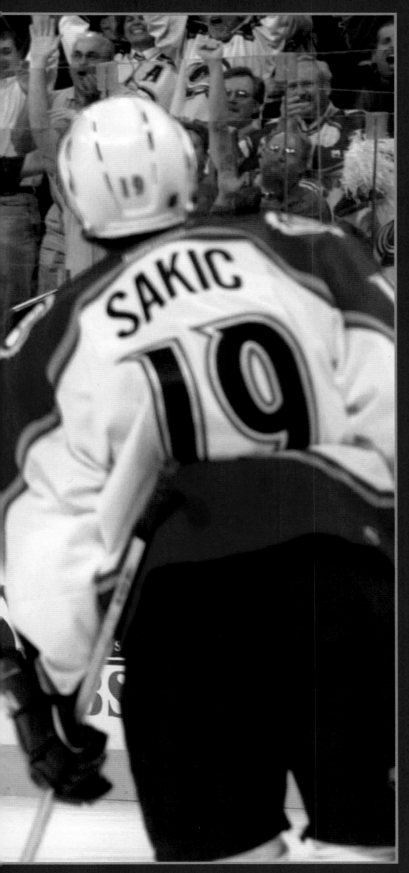

GAME 7

May 9 at Colorado

Avalanche   5
Kings   1

This was the most pressure-filled game in Avalanche history.

If the Avs had blown their three games-to-one lead against the Kings and exited the playoffs after the second round, coach Bob Hartley probably wouldn't have retained his job. It also would have been difficult to justify maintaining an upper-echelon payroll, meaning the Avs would be hard-pressed to keep all their unrestricted free agents.

So if a few players were squeezing their sticks in Game 7 against the Kings, it wouldn't have been a shock. But the Avalanche came through, scoring four times in the third period to break a 1-1 tie.

Chris Drury, Ville Nieminen and Shjon Podein scored for the Avs in the third before Milan Hejduk finished it off with an empty-net goal with 3:35 remaining in regulation.

Rob Blake scored the Avs' first goal on a first-period power play.

"There are a lot of guys in here who have been in a lot of big-game situations, and a lot of guys who know how to get the job done in pressure situations," Blake said after Colorado's 5-1 triumph. "That's what they did tonight."

Patrick Roy had 25 saves and limited Los Angeles to one goal for the third consecutive game. Ray Bourque scored his first points of the postseason with two assists.

After the game, Peter Forsberg, who had scored four goals and collected 10 assists so far in the 2001 playoffs, peered playfully around the corner from the players'

TAKE-ALL GAME 7 OF THE AVS-KINGS SERIES.

GAME 7

dressing area, wrapped two towels around himself, entered the locker-room area and did a handful of interviews. He was laughing and joking with reporters.

Two hours later, Forsberg was doubled over in pain at a Denver restaurant. He was rushed to Rose Medical Center and, in the middle of the night, underwent surgery to remove his spleen. Later, neither Forsberg nor anyone else could pinpoint anything that happened in Game 7—or earlier—that could have triggered the problem.

The Avs would have to make do without Forsberg for the rest of their playoff run. However long it might last.

KINGS COACH ANDY MURRAY SHOUTED ENCOURAGEMENT TO HIS PLAYERS, WHO HAD REASON TO MAKE A LITTLE NOISE OF THEIR OWN (TOP) AFTER TYING GAME 7 AT 1-1.

Los Angeles' Felix Potvin and Mattias Norstrom watched the bouncing puck off the stick of Rob Blake cross the goal line. The Avs broke loose for four more goals, one of them by Ville Nieminen (above).

ROUND

3

9W

10W

11W

12W

GAME 1

May 12 at Colorado

Avalanche	4
Blues	1

THREW HIS STICK TRYING TO MAKE A SAVE.

The Avalanche entered the first game of the Western Conference finals against a rested St. Louis Blues team that had just swept two-time defending conference champion Dallas. The Avs, meanwhile, needed seven games to dispatch Los Angeles. And now Colorado was without superstar Peter Forsberg, who underwent season-ending spleen surgery after Game 7 of the Western semifinals.

At this point, the Avs were being written off by armchair pundits.

Someone forgot to inform the doubters that the sum of this Avalanche team was greater than its parts. Even without Forsberg, and with captain Joe Sakic still unable to take faceoffs because of a sore right shoulder, the Avs throttled the Blues, 4-1, in Game 1 at the Pepsi Center.

Sakic was the hero, scoring two goals and assisting on the others. The enduring image from Game 1 was Sakic's penalty-shot goal against Blues goalie Roman Turek, who didn't have a chance on Sakic's laser of a wrist shot to the right corner. The goal electrified the Pepsi Center, and Turek seemed rattled. He would seem that way for the rest of the series, in fact.

Patrick Roy allowed only a Scott Young short-handed goal to start what would be a dominant performance in the series.

As long as Roy played the way he did, if the Avs could get enough offense from their first line and if the big three defensive core of Ray Bourque, Rob Blake and Adam Foote could shut down the other team's first line,

GAME 1

the team came to the realization that maybe, just maybe, it could win without Forsberg.

There would be plenty of stiff tests ahead, but winning this game did wonders for the Avalanche's psyche.

"That first game against the Blues was very important," Roy would say later. "It gave us a lot of confidence in ourselves."

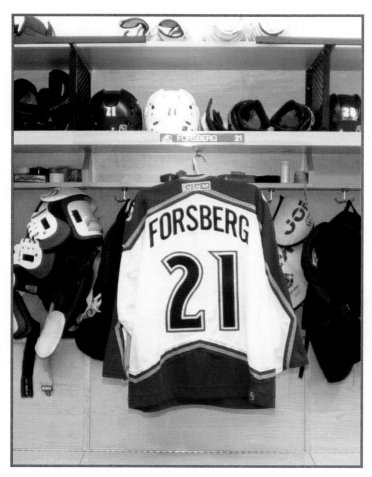

THE REST OF THE PLAYOFFS WOULD BE PLAYED WITHOUT THE SERVICES OF PETER FORSBERG. MILAN HEJDUK CORRALLED A LOOSE PUCK IN THE SLOT AND SLID IT PAST ROMAN TUREK (TOP).

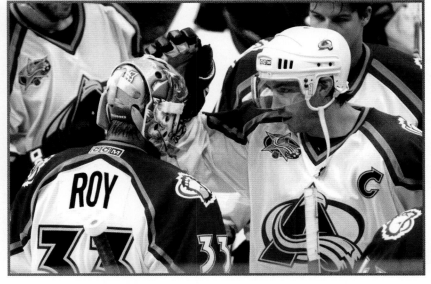

Body-crunching checks, such as the one Shjon Podein put on Marty Reasoner (above), set the tone for the remainder of the series. Joe Sakic had two goals and two assists to spark the Avalanche offense. Meanwhile, Patrick Roy held his ground in net, allowing only one goal to the Blues.

With Alex Tanguay screening him, Roman Turek had no chance on Ray Bourque's first-period shot.

GAME 2

May 14 at Colorado

| Avalanche | 4 |
| Blues | 2 |

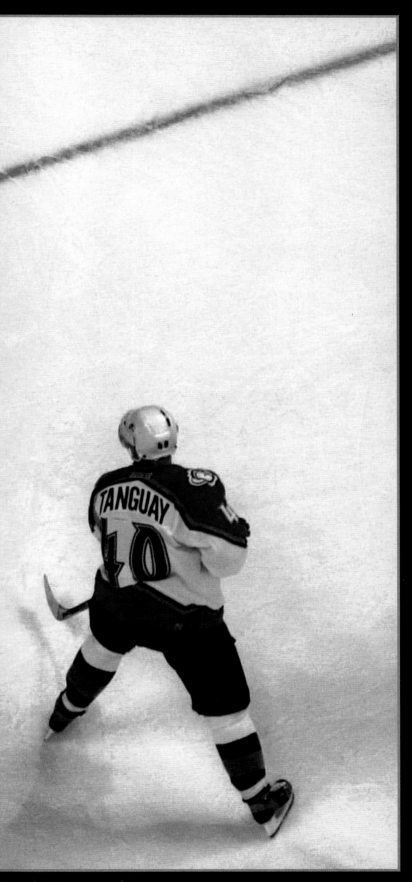

Ray Bourque hadn't collected a goal in the 2001 playoffs entering Game 2, but he changed that in the first period with a slap shot past Roman Turek. That set the tone for the night, as the Avs again made the most of their chances and Patrick Roy frustrated the Blues' talented forwards at the other end.

Blues veteran Scott Mellanby tied the game in the second period with a pretty tip past Roy, but normally light-scoring Avs defenseman Adam Foote got the lead back with another slap shot past Turek.

Of the many things Bourque taught Foote after Bourque's arrival from Boston late in the 1999-2000 season, perhaps the most important was that it was OK to shoot the puck on net. Foote, who mostly had been a stay-at-home defenseman, credited Bourque with making him more comfortable when it came to looking for offensive opportunities.

Shjon Podein scored the back-breaking goal against the Blues in the third period when he burst down the right side of St. Louis' zone and beat Turek with a short shot to the near post, making it 3-1. Podein scored a handful of similar goals during the season.

Al MacInnis cut the lead to 3-2 at 15:52 of the period, but the Blues lost any chance at a comeback when veteran center Pierre Turgeon foolishly slashed Foote in the back of his knee with about a minute to go, leaving the Blues shorthanded.

St. Louis had been coming on at that point, but Turgeon's penalty allowed Chris Drury to seal the game

GAME 2

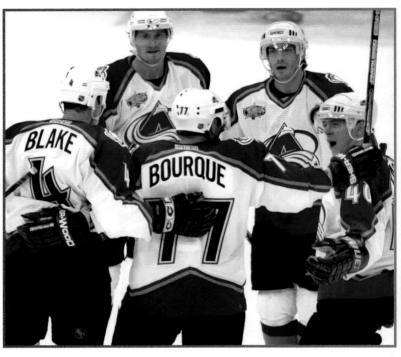

at 4-2 with an empty-net goal. The Peter Forsberg-less Avs now had a two-games-to-none lead against the favored Blues. Everybody seemed surprised—except the Avalanche.

"We got what we wanted from the first two games," said Roy, who made 28 saves. "Now, we know it's going to be a lot tougher in St. Louis."

RAY BOURQUE'S FIRST-PERIOD GOAL GAVE THE AVALANCHE AN EARLY LEAD AND PATRICK ROY PLAYED ANOTHER SOLID, IF NOT SPECTACULAR, GAME TO GIVE THE AVS A 2-0 SERIES LEAD.

Although St. Louis had plenty of traffic in front of Patrick Roy (top) he was still able to notch yet another playoff victory. Shjon Podein (left) poked the puck past Blues goalie Roman Turek as he skated behind the net, making the score 3-1. Podein's shot proved to be the winning goal for Game 2.

SEAN HILL SENDS A LEFT-HANDER TO DAN HINOTE AND AWAITS HIS RESPONSE.

GAME 3

May 16 at St. Louis

Blues	4
Avalanche	3

(2 OT)

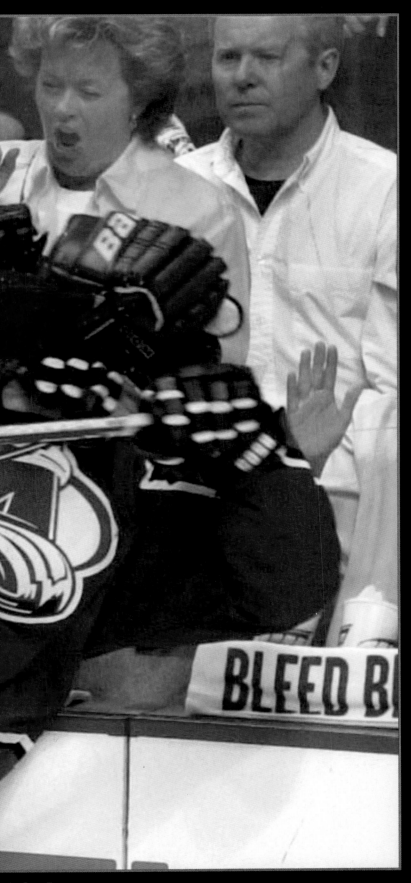

A St. Louis victory cut the series lead in half.

I t was muggy and uncomfortable in St. Louis on the day of Game 3. And by game's end, players on both sides appeared on the verge of dehydration. Patrick Roy simply wouldn't let anyone go home on time.

But as much as the Avalanche goalie tried to pull one out for his team, it just didn't happen. Scott Young's wrist shot at 10:27 of the second overtime got the Blues back into this series with a 4-3 victory.

This was a game the Avalanche didn't deserve to win—but should have anyway. Despite being outshot nearly 2-1 by the Blues, the Avs appeared certain of victory and a 3-0 series lead in the first overtime when center Stephane Yelle had the puck on his stick with a wide-open net in front of him.

Blues goalie Roman Turek was out of position after mishandling a long dump-in to the Blues' zone, and all Yelle had to do was put a backhander in from about five feet to win it. But Turek managed to get enough of his stick on the puck to make it hit the far post, and the Avs never did mount much more of an assault on Turek, who had been shaky throughout the game.

After the Blues took their first lead of the series early in the first period, Ray Bourque and Dan Hinote scored back-to-back goals. Hinote's backhander was the result of another Turek misplay on a dump-in, and Blues fans began to shower the goalie with boos.

After the Blues tied it, Eric Messier gave Colorado a 3-2 lead in the third period, which seemed safe with Roy in goal. But the Blues' Jamal Mayers scored with

GAME 3

5:43 left to tie it again.

Young decided matters after taking a Pierre Turgeon pass and beating Roy up high.

The Blues left the building tired but happy after out-shooting the Avalanche, 60-33, and dominating most aspects of the game. The Avs, meanwhile, couldn't help but think they had blown a great chance at stealing one.

"I know I'm probably not going to sleep very well tonight," a dejected Yelle said.

ROMAN TUREK'S MISHANDLING OF THE PUCK (ABOVE) LED TO DAN HINOTE'S GOAL. KEITH TKACHUK AND ADAM FOOTE (RIGHT) FIGHT FOR POSITION.

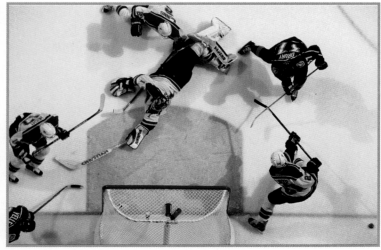

STEPHANE YELLE HAD AN OPEN-NET CHANCE TO PUT THE GAME AWAY IN THE FIRST OVERTIME (ABOVE, LEFT), BUT ROMAN TUREK DIVED AND JUST GOT A PIECE OF THE PUCK WITH HIS STICK, FORCING IT WIDE OF THE FAR POST (ABOVE). THAT SET THE TABLE FOR FORMER AVALANCHE WINGER SCOTT YOUNG TO SCORE THE GAME-WINNER AT 10:27 OF THE SECOND OVER-TIME. YOUNG BEAT PATRICK ROY WITH A WRIST SHOT OVER HIS RIGHT SHOULDER TO GIVE THE BLUES THEIR FIRST WIN OF THE SERIES.

GAME 4

May 18 at St. Louis

Avalanche	4	
Blues	3	(OT)

Redemption. Payback. From goat to hero. From the outhouse to the penthouse.

Hockey writers everywhere were hauling out time-worn cliches to describe Stephane Yelle's short stay in NHL purgatory. Just two nights after failing to score on an empty net in overtime, Yelle didn't miss when given another chance in overtime of Game 4. The result was a 4-3 Avalanche victory and a 3-1 series lead for Colorado.

Yelle scored 13 goals in 1995-96, his rookie season with the Avs, but he had failed to crack the double-figure mark since. After his big miss in Game 3, confidence seemed in short supply for the quiet Ottawa native.

But Yelle had a grin from ear to ear after taking Rob Blake's crossing pass and knocking it past Roman Turek at 4:23 of overtime. Yelle not only improved his standing with Avs fans, he rescued a team that nearly blew a game that appeared in the bag after the first period.

Colorado scored three goals on Turek in a span of 78 seconds. Steve Reinprecht scored his first career playoff goal to get things started, and then Joe Sakic and Ray Bourque beat Turek with back-to-back, long-range shots. The Blues were stunned, and fans booed Turek when he was temporarily replaced by Brent Johnson.

But the Avs, as they have done on occasion, sat back and watched the Blues claw back into the game. Pierre Turgeon scored twice to cut it to 3-2, and when the Blues evened the score just 58 seconds into the third period, the Avs seemed in real danger.

GAME 4

But Colorado stayed tough, with Patrick Roy making several amazing saves, and sent the game into overtime. Roy's best save was a glove stop of a Scott Young blast from the slot late in regulation.

"I don't know how he got that one," Young said.

But Roy got it. And Stephane Yelle got a big one, too.

ROB BLAKE (ABOVE) MADE SCOTT YOUNG PAY THE PRICE IN A HARD-FOUGHT GAME. RAY BOURQUE (RIGHT) REACTED TO SCORING HIS TEAM'S THIRD GOAL OF THE FIRST PERIOD.

St. Louis fought back (above) as Bryce Salvador leveled Dan Hinote. The Blues celebrated Jamal Mayers' third-period goal that tied the game, but their joy was short-lived.

GAME 5

May 21 at Colorado

Avalanche	2	(OT)
Blues	1	

I n each of the previous two seasons, the Avalanche had a chance to win Game 7 of the Western Conference title series and advance to the Stanley Cup Finals, but Ed Belfour and the Dallas Stars said no.

This time, Belfour was at home in his Barcalounger, and Roman Turek was the goalie standing in the way.

Or so the Avs thought, until Blues coach Joel Quenneville decided to replace Turek for Game 5 with rookie Brent Johnson, a one-time Avalanche farmhand.

When the game was over, many Blues fans were asking, "Why didn't Quenneville put Johnson in sooner?"

Johnson nearly sent the series back to St. Louis, making several top-notch saves in regulation and allowing only a second-period goal by Milan Hejduk. Bryce Salvador scored on Patrick Roy, and the Blues—in a 1-1 tie—appeared to have a good shot at upending an Avs team that was starting to look very frustrated against Johnson. In fact, the Avs had the same look on their faces as they did against Belfour.

But then, late in regulation, the Avs were given a power-play opportunity, one that carried over into the extra period. Before any Avs fans could start biting their fingernails, Joe Sakic ended it all.

Just 24 seconds into the extra period, Rob Blake skated toward Johnson from the right circle and fired a shot that the St. Louis goalie stopped. Sakic saw the puck come to his stick and, with a sizable target in front of him, tapped it into the net.

Finally, the Avs had gotten back to the Stanley Cup Finals—where they hadn't been since winning it all in 1996

AVALANCHE TO THE STANLEY CUP FINALS.

GAME 5

BRENT JOHNSON WAS A SURPRISE STARTER IN GOAL FOR THE BLUES IN GAME 5. BUT THERE WERE NO SURPRISES IN THE AVS' NET AS PATRICK ROY AGAIN WAS STELLAR, ROBBING PAVOL DEMITRA (RIGHT).

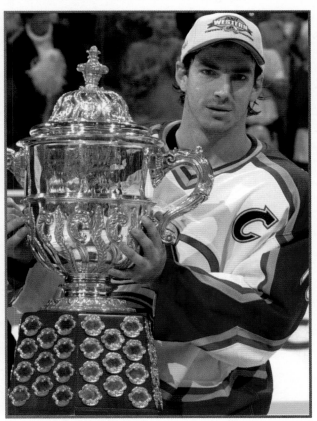

The Avs finally got a shot past Brent Johnson as Milan Hejduk scored in the second period. Joe Sakic (left) accepted the Clarence Campbell Trophy, which is awarded to the Western Conference champions.

ROUND
4

13W

14W

15W

16W

PATRICK ROY MADE AN EARLY STATEMENT IN THE FINALS WITH HIS GAME 1 SHUTOUT. HE WAS ABLE TO KEEP

GAME 1

May 26 at Colorado

Avalanche	5
Devils	0

Coming into the Stanley Cup finals, Colorado Avalanche players were determined to control the puck in the neutral zone against the defensively aggressive New Jersey Devils. And they wanted to crash the net.

As it turned out, the Avs were successful on both counts.

The Avalanche played an almost flawless game and won nearly every battle in the neutral zone on its way to a shocking 5-0 win over the reigning champs in Game 1 of the Stanley Cup Finals.

New Jersey had difficulty in the neutral zone. As a result, the Avs were able to gather speed and turn it into heavy-duty crease crashing against Devils goaltender Martin Brodeur.

"We watched a lot of tape of their Toronto series," Avalanche center Joe Sakic said. "We saw how Toronto used speed to get in and forecheck them and crash the net. We felt we could use our speed wide, get the puck behind their defense and then go to the net.

"We obviously had our legs tonight, and our speed was key. But we still feel that this is just one game and we are worried about how well they play in the neutral zone. If we can continue to use simple plays and get it behind their 'D' and use our speed, we will be OK."

To a man, the Avs said before the series they felt they had to get the puck in deep against the Devils and use their speed to create offense down low. A little crunching against the boards wouldn't hurt, either.

And that's exactly what they did.

SNIPERS SUCH AS JOHN MADDEN (11) OFF THE SCOREBOARD

GAME 1

"Our guys were getting hit left and right," Devils coach Larry Robinson said. "We didn't do a good job of obstructing them and holding them up from getting in and getting on the forecheck."

Sakic and his teammates continued to stress the importance of not making mistakes in the neutral zone because of the Devils' tremendously quick transition game that helped them get to the Finals.

"You have to take the play to them," Sakic said. "If you let them take it to you, they're going to do some damage."

The Avs had the play taken to them in the past. In the last two playoffs, the Dallas Stars had been successful by forcing the Avs' smaller forwards wide by clogging the middle of the ice in their zone and making Colorado take bad-percentage shots from the perimeter. So it would seem logical for New Jersey to try that plan as well.

But the Devils didn't have it in place in Game 1, and the goals were proof of that.

■ Sakic's first goal, his 10th of the playoffs, came at 11:07 of the first period after he passed Devils defenseman Scott Stevens at the blue line and then used his speed to get around winger Sergei Nemchinov. The goal came while Sakic swooped in on net from the left-wing faceoff circle.

■ Sandwiched between two successful Avalanche penalty-kills was Chris Drury's goal, which came at 9:35 of the second period. The Avs took advantage of the Devils by moving the puck around quickly. In a bing-bang-boom play, Ville Nieminen moved the puck to Dan Hinote, who hit Drury with a nice pass just as Drury was zipping across the crease, for the perfect redirection. The quick puck movement was another way the

THE AVS BROUGHT THEIR 'A'
GAME TO THE FINALS OPENER.
CHRIS DRURY CHIPPED IN A
GOAL AND ROB BLAKE ADDED A
GOAL AND TWO ASSISTS. DAN
HINOTE CONTINUED TO PLAY
PHYSICAL HOCKEY, AND HE GOT
ON THE SCORE SHEET IN GAME 1
BY ASSISTING ON DRURY'S GOAL.
JOE SAKIC COLLECTED TWO
GOALS FOR COLORADO, ONE
COMING AS ALEXANDER
MOGILNY WATCHED HELPLESSLY.

GAME 1

Avs were faster than the Devils on this night.

■ Sakic's second goal of the game, coming with 4:54 left in the second period, was made possible by Alex Tanguay's drive for the net.

During a 4-on-4, Sakic took advantage of a Devils miscommunication and a stumbling Stevens to dodge across the slot and beat Brodeur, who was knocked over by Petr Sykora, who had been pushed there by Alex Tanguay. With Brodeur knocked backward, Sakic gave the Avalanche a seemingly insurmountable 3-0 lead. It was another example of the Devils appearing mystified as to how to slow down the dynamic Avalanche. Stevens, especially, seemed vulnerable: He was minus-3 through the first two periods.

■ Defenseman Rob Blake added the fourth goal, scoring on the power play 5:36 into the third period with Turner Stevenson in the box for goaltender interference. Blake left his right-point position to take a perfect one-timer from the faceoff circle, before completing a pretty passing play by Tanguay, who was circling the net. The goal came just after a holding penalty to Hinote had expired.

■ Steven Reinprecht circled in front of the net untouched by Devils defender Ken Daneyko to complete the scoring with 2:24 left.

The Avs no longer have in-your-face power forwards such as Claude Lemieux, Mike Ricci or Adam Deadmarsh from their 1996 Stanley Cup title team, but unless the Devils really get hard-nosed in front of Brodeur in the rest of the series, they might be looking at a one-year Stanley Cup reign.

"We caused lots of turnovers," Avs coach Bob Hartley said. "Our pressure was great ... Tonight we took advantage of them."

ALEX TANGUAY CONTINUALLY CRASHED THE NET, BUT IT

WAS JOE SAKIC'S TWO GOALS THAT LED THE AVALANCHE TO A VICTORY IN GAME I.

ERIC MESSIER WAS ON THE RECEIVING END OF SOME OF THE PHYSICAL PLAY IN GAME 2, AS THE NEW JERSEY

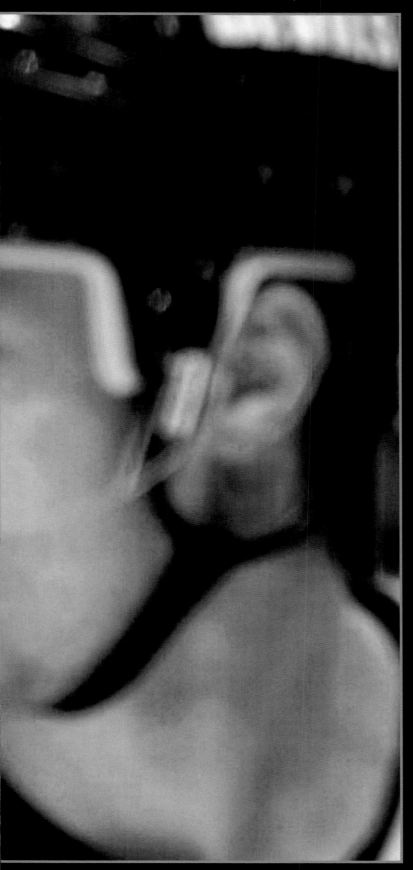

GAME 2

May 29 at Colorado

| Devils | 2 |
| Avalanche | 1 |

The real New Jersey Devils decided to show up for Game 2.

The Devils stuck to the game plan that had made them the top team in the Eastern Conference (111 points) and seized a 2-1 win over the Avalanche to tie the Stanley Cup Finals at one game each.

The instructions for the Devils before the game were simple:

■ Clog the middle in the neutral zone and the front of their own net to force the quicker Avalanche to the perimeter. React faster and quicken the pace of your game.

■ Match and exceed the Avalanche's intensity.

■ Hit and be aggressive.

Not on the blackboard: get goals from unexpected sources Bob Corkum and Turner Stevenson, neither of whom had scored a playoff goal before Game 2.

The Devils covered all the strategic points, dramatically raising their game to a level that helped them make up for their embarrassing 5-0 loss in Game 1.

But Corkum and Stevenson? They sound more like a third-party campaign ticket than the two players who threatened to light a fire under the Devils by scoring less than 3 minutes apart late in the first period. The goals came after Joe Sakic once again provided the Avalanche with an early lead by netting a power-play goal 5:58 into the game.

"It's like two singles hitters hitting home runs in the World Series, isn't it?" Stevenson said. "If you had a

DEVILS CAME OUT PLAYING 'IN YOUR FACE' HOCKEY.

GAME 2

JOE SAKIC HAD NOW SCORED THREE GOALS IN JUST THE FIRST TWO GAMES OF THE FINALS. MEANWHILE, THE DEVILS GOT OFFENSE FROM UNLIKELY SOURCES. BOB CORKUM AND TURNER STEVENSON SCORED IN THE FIRST PERIOD, GIVING THE DEVILS THE LEAD.

pool on who would get the winning goal, I don't know anyone who would have picked me."

Corkum was inserted into the lineup after right winger Randy McKay fractured his left hand during a collision with Ray Bourque early in the second period of Game 1.

Corkum had one assist in six playoff games this year and has scored 87 goals in 570 career games over 10 NHL seasons. He had just seven goals this season in 75 games with the Los Angeles Kings and the Devils. Corkum had been put on waivers by the Kings before the Devils made a late trade for him, mainly to help on faceoffs, so he was an unlikely hero.

Corkum's goal came on a partial breakaway, with Martin Skoula in hot pursuit. Corkum fired off a quick snap shot, beating Patrick Roy between the legs.

"Someone asked me if I knew how close (Avs defenseman) Martin Skoula was to me when I got the breakaway," Corkum says. "I don't know, I was just looking ahead of me. There's no way I was going to look back."

And the Devils never looked back after Corkum's goal.

The goal picked up the Devils' spirits, and after scoring they seemed willing to buy into coach Larry Robinson's plan of putting two red shirts in front of Roy on the attack. After failing to score on a rare five-on-three playoff power play, the Devils collected the go-ahead goal by jamming the front. The crowd didn't gather right on Roy's doorstep, as you might expect, more on his front lawn, between the hash marks.

Once there, the two Devils attempted to deflect shots and go after rebounds.

"We can't expect to compete unless we are the

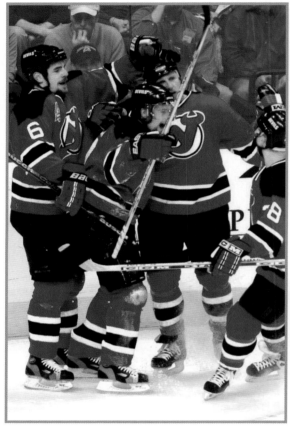

SPACE WAS AT A PREMIUM ON BOTH ENDS OF THE ICE, AS THE AVALANCHE DEFENDERS KEPT THE FRONT OF THE NET CLEAR FOR PATRICK ROY, BUT THE DAMAGE HAD ALREADY BEEN DONE. AFTER THEIR FIRST-PERIOD GOAL, THE AVALANCHE PLAYERS COULDN'T FIND A WAY TO GET ANY OFFENSIVE PRESSURE ON DEVILS GOALIE MARTIN BRODEUR. THE COACHING STAFF AND PLAYERS WERE LEFT LOOKING FOR ANSWERS.

GAME 2

aggressors," Devils captain Scott Stevens said. "They put us back on our heels with their speed in Game 1. We knew we had to return the favor tonight.

"When we are assertive and don't stand back and wait, our defense in the neutral zone is better and we wind up outhitting and outshooting opponents."

The tactic worked perfectly on Stevenson's goal. After Scott Niedermayer's shot was stopped by Avs defenseman Jon Klemm in front, Stevenson batted at the stalled puck to beat Roy for what would be the game-winner.

Stevenson was an equally unlikely hero: He had 45 goals in 385 games in eight NHL seasons before this one and had only eight goals in 69 games for the Devils this season.

The Devils' deadly transition game also looked a lot sharper, much sharper than in the debacle that was Game 1.

"We moved the puck up better and forced (them) to turn the puck over," Stevens said. "We made their defense work and tried to put more pressure on their three (top) guys."

Game 2 is what everyone expected at the outset of the series. Not necessarily a Devils victory, but a battle for every inch of the ice from the first faceoff to the final buzzer.

"We knew they were going to be able to adjust," Roy said. "They're the defending champions."

It has been 54 years since a team lost by more than four goals in Game 1 and came back to win the Stanley Cup, which had been won 79 percent of the time by the team taking the first game.

The Devils had adjusted, and now they were acclimated as well. Your move, Bob Hartley.

Martin Brodeur played a steady game, making 19 saves. Bobby Holik continued his physical play and made his presence known along the boards. The Avalanche defensemen continued to shoot the puck at the net, hoping to create rebounds, but the Devils made sure no one could make it to the loose pucks in time. Turner Stevenson's first goal of the playoffs proved to be the game-winner.

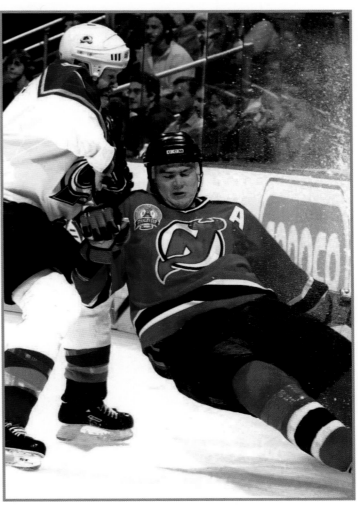

MARTIN BRODEUR COULDN'T DO ANYTHING BUT WATCH AS THE THIRD GOAL OF THE GAME WENT IN. IT WAS

DAN HINOTE'S SECOND GOAL OF THE PLAYOFFS.

GAME 3

May 31 at New Jersey

Avalanche	3
Devils	1

Forget the fancy plays. In this Stanley Cup Finals matchup, there's just not enough room for those to develop.

What that means, then, is hand-to-hand combat—more precisely, getting traffic in front of the net. The Devils' defensemen had taken that away from the Avalanche in Game 2.

Where there's a will, there's a way. And the determination of Colorado forwards Alex Tanguay and Milan Hejduk—along with the checking line of Stephane Yelle, Shjon Podein and Dave Reid—to go to the net clearly gave the Avalanche plenty of opportunities in Game 3.

More important, with the traffic in front of the net and the checking so tight, defensemen often become the key. A particularly important defenseman turned out to be Colorado's Ray Bourque, who stepped up from the blue line and drilled a shot past Devils goaltender Martin Brodeur on a power play 31 seconds into the third period. That goal pushed the Avalanche ahead by a 2-1 score en route to a 3-1 victory at Continental Airlines Arena in Game 3 of this series.

"Part of our game plan was for the defensemen to be active," Bourque said. "There wasn't much room in front or around the net, but there was a little room to move the puck from the blue line in for the 'D.'

"On the winning goal, Joe (Sakic) won the draw and we got a screen in front of Marty and I just tried to get it up, figuring that he would have to go down to try to get a better look at the play with all of the traffic in

GAME 3

front of him."

Playing in his 22nd NHL season with all sorts of awards but no Stanley Cup, Bourque holds the dubious distinction of playing the most games without winning the NHL championship.

On this night, at age 40, Bourque became the oldest player to score a goal in the Stanley Cup Finals, breaking the record of Montreal legend Jean Beliveau (39).

So, Ray, how did this goal rank with all of your memories?

"With just two wins away from the Stanley Cup," he said, smiling, "I don't think I've ever scored a bigger goal. I know it made me feel like I was about 25 instead of 40."

Midway through the first period, with the Devils ahead, 1-0, thanks to a power-play goal by Jason Arnott, Avalanche defenseman Martin Skoula was the hero as he moved into the slot and lifted a shot behind Brodeur at the 10:38 mark, with Podein playing the role of the foot soldier creating havoc in front of the net.

And later in the third period, a great outlet pass from the defense helped second-line center Chris Drury get a three-on-two, odd-man rush against New Jersey that resulted in a tick-tack-toe passing play from Drury to Ville Nieminen to Dan Hinote, who scored 6:28 into the period.

"We knew we would have to support each other in all three zones, otherwise there's no room at all against the Devils," Avalanche coach Bob Hartley said. "We weren't going to get the outnumbered situations we wanted without bringing the defensemen up into the play."

Counting the goals by Skoula and Bourque, Avalanche defensemen had scored 13 of the team's 59

Joe Sakic didn't have much room to operate in during Game 3. But other players picked up the scoring slack. Martin Skoula tied the game, 1-1, in the first period with his first goal of the playoffs as Stephane Yelle and Shjon Podein screened Martin Brodeur.

GAME 3

goals in the 2000-01 playoffs—a clear and potent weapon that the Devils hadn't been able to match so far in the series.

"Every time I looked up, one of their defensemen seemed to have the puck and was moving closer and closer toward the net," Brodeur says. "We're going to have to clog up the middle of the ice in our zone again like we did in Game 2 and hopefully get a lead and frustrate them again."

The Devils had taken the initiative early in the first period, and their pressure forced Avalanche defenseman Adam Foote to take a penalty. On the ensuing power play, New Jersey moved the puck quickly from the right-wing corner to the left-wing faceoff circle for a one-timer by point man Arnott, who caught Colorado goaltender Patrick Roy going from side to side. The puck got between Roy's pads, and New Jersey had a 1-0 lead just 3:16 into the game.

With Patrik Elias getting an assist on the play, it represented the first points of the series by the Devils' No. 1 line. Whereas the Devils' six-man defense was key to winning Game 2, the Avalanche's defense—headed by the Big Three of Bourque, Rob Blake and Adam Foote, plus Skoula, Jon Klemm and Greg deVries—clearly made the difference in this game. And by moving the puck quickly and stepping up whenever possible, the Colorado defense created the room it wasn't allowed in Game 2.

In the process, the Avalanche regained the home-ice advantage at the Devils' arena, where they had posted a record of 0-4-2 since 1995 and a mark of 0-6-2 going back a year earlier when the team was known as the Quebec Nordiques and had no Stanley Cup Finals history whatsoever.

RAY BOURQUE (LEFT AND BOTTOM), 40, BECAME THE OLDEST PLAYER TO SCORE A GOAL IN THE STANLEY CUP FINALS. PATRICK ROY STOPPED 21 OF 22 SHOTS TO PRESERVE GAME 3 FOR COLORADO.

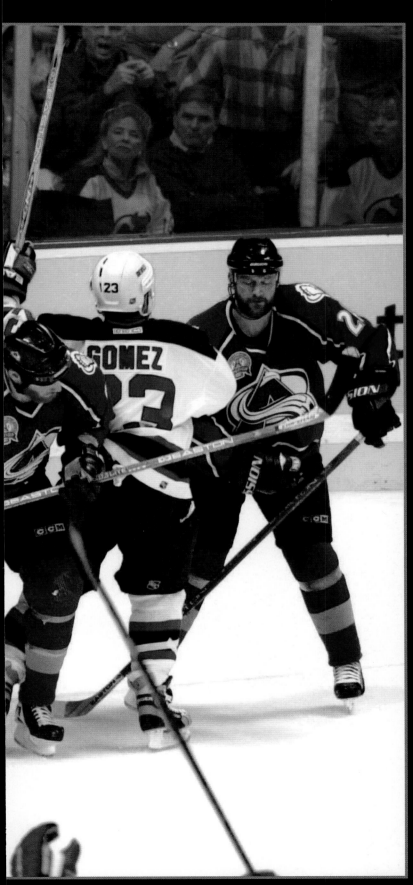

GAME 4

June 2 at New Jersey

Devils	3
Avalanche	2

Get it deep. Avoid stupid penalties. Match the Avalanche's intensity. Create offense. Stop Joe Sakic.

In other words, two nights after the Avalanche had defeated New Jersey with a Devils-like approach to the game (stingy and tight-checking defense), the Devils would attempt to win Game 4 by playing their patented style.

Taken aside by coach Larry Robinson at a team-only meeting held earlier in the day and in no uncertain terms being told this was a must-win situation, the Devils obviously paid close attention. They prevailed, 3-2, and evened the Stanley Cup Finals at two victories apiece.

In the end, the Devils showed their physical side big time in the third period as Bobby Holik put Milan Hejduk out of the game with a hard, blind-side shoulder check and captain Scott Stevens began to deliver some of his famous hard hits (twice sending Sakic to the ice).

That kind of physical play helped New Jersey get the puck in deep against the Avalanche—and it enabled the Devils to overcome a 2-1 deficit after two periods. Goals by Scott Gomez and Petr Sykora won it for New Jersey.

"We had great passion, great jump," said Robinson, who criticized his team for, in effect, not showing up for Game 3.

Robinson's team got big contributions from Patrik Elias, Gomez and Sykora. Elias scored on a shorthanded goal, Gomez collected his first goal in 13 playoffs games and Sykora notched the game-winner with 2:37 left in

OF A PUCK BEHIND THE NET CHANGED ALL THAT.

GAME 4

the game.

Gomez's goal came 8:09 into the third period on a gaffe by Avs goaltender Patrick Roy, who had strayed out of position and was unable to scramble back. Jay Pandolfo retrieved a loose puck and sent it in front to Gomez, who backhanded it into an empty net.

Then, after the hits by Holik and Stevens, Elias held the puck in the Colorado zone on an attempted clearing pass by Avs defenseman Rob Blake. Holik held the puck along the left-wing boards until Elias again retrieved it and found Sykora standing in the slot alone for a one-timer and a telling goal.

Befitting a Finals, big-time momentum was swinging back and forth.

It was New Jersey that came out strong in this game and missed on a great scoring opportunity by Turner Stevenson. Colorado came right back up the ice after Roy's save on Stevenson, and Blake used his speed to get a step on Stevens and moved in on goaltender Martin Brodeur for a goal just 3:58 into the game.

New Jersey players didn't heed their coach's advice about penalties and put the Avalanche on three power plays in the first half of the first period that resulted in a 1-0 Colorado lead. But the second period belonged to the Devils, as New Jersey held a 19-8 edge in shots through 40 minutes.

Elias tied the game, 1-1, when he scored a shorthanded goal on Roy just 3:42 into the second period. The Devils had numerous other chances to score as well.

But give the Avalanche credit for handling the pressure and getting another clutch goal from prime-time center Chris Drury, who took a Chris Dingman pass in the center-ice neutral zone and powered his way

ROB BLAKE GAVE THE AVALANCHE AN EARLY LEAD WITH HIS FIRST-PERIOD GOAL. SCOTT GOMEZ, WHO HADN'T SCORED A GOAL IN HIS LAST 12 GAMES, TRIED TO MAKE A DROP PASS AT COLORADO'S BLUE LINE.

GAME 4

around New Jersey defenseman Sean O'Donnell and in alone on Brodeur. Drury deposited the shot through a small hole along the ice with just 6:06 left in the second period.

"I told the players this morning at our team-only meeting that this is not the time where you can wait for a guy or for a player to get out of a slump or to start playing better," Robinson said. "You have to make decisions right off the bat because you are running out of tomorrows.

"I said there will be no tomorrow because the Avalanche never quit, they've got great speed and they beat us at our own game in Game 3—and that is not acceptable."

Robinson's response to being out-Deviled by Colorado in Game 3 was to move Holik into a checking assignment on Sakic in an effort to free center Jason Arnott's No. 1 line from a checking role to a scoring role after Sakic's line had outscored Arnott's eight points to two in the first three games of the Finals.

As it turned out, Arnott wasn't a factor after he was hit by a puck high in the left side of the head on his first shift of the game.

But Elias and Sykora were major factors, and so was the previously invisible Gomez.

"It took everything we had to get it behind Patrick Roy," Gomez said. "We knew we'd have to keep coming at them in waves for 60 minutes to give ourselves a chance to win the game against him.

"And that's exactly what we're going to have to give again (in Game 5).

"Sixty minutes again. And no excuses for anything less."

CHRIS DRURY SCORED IN THE SECOND PERIOD, COLLECTING HIS 10TH GOAL OF THE PLAYOFFS. RAY BOURQUE SURVEYED WHAT WAS GOING ON BEHIND HIM.

GAME 4 PROVED TO BE A BATTLE OF THE GOALTENDERS. BUT PATRICK ROY'S POOR HANDLING OF THE PUCK ALLOWED THE DEVILS TO COME BACK. MARTIN BRODEUR MADE SURE THE ONE-GOAL LEAD HELD UP. THE DEVILS WON, 3-2, AND TIED THE SERIES AT 2-2.

With eight odd-man chances in the game, New Jersey took advantage of the opportunities and

GAME 5

June 4 at Colorado

Devils	4
Avalanche	1

SCORED FOUR TIMES ON PATRICK ROY.

To the precipice.

That's where the Devils pushed the Avalanche by winning Game 5 of the Stanley Cup Finals and taking a three-games-to-two lead in the best-of-seven series.

New Jersey's Patrik Elias opened the scoring when he and Petr Sykora broke in on one of four odd-man breaks the Devils got in the first period against the usually tight Colorado defense. Elias' goal came just 3:09 into the game.

New Jersey wound up with eight odd-man breaks in Game 5, compared with just two for the Avalanche. The speed of New Jersey finally showed through and, really, it was just as impressive in this game as Colorado's quickness had been in the first four games.

"I can't explain the reason we got caught in way too many odd-man rushes," Avalanche coach Bob Hartley said after the Devils' 4-1 victory. "Maybe we were too anxious."

In what had become a series of momentum switches, the Avalanche came back at the 10:09 mark to score a power-play goal when Alex Tanguay beat New Jersey on a 3-on-1 against Martin Brodeur. The goal came seconds after Ray Bourque had broken up a 3-on-2 short-handed opportunity as Devils defenseman Scott Niedermayer got caught up the ice.

More odd-man rushes were to follow.

With the game tied, 1-1, and time running out in the first period, the Devils' Scott Gomez took a quick transitional feed from defenseman Brian Rafalski. He

GAME 5

then dropped a pass to Alexander Mogilny, who completed a 3-on-1 with a quick wrist shot low to Patrick Roy's stick side with just 1:13 remaining before the intermission.

This was the same Scott Gomez who had gone 12 games without a goal before scoring the tying goal in the Devils' 3-2 victory in Game 4. And before Game 5, Mogilny had gone 14 games without netting a goal.

"I thought I might have to retire," Mogilny joked after the long slump that followed a team-high 43 goals in the regular season. "Seriously, seeing Scott get his goal in the last game helped give me more confidence to just go out there and start shooting."

Mogilny wound up with four shots on goal in the game, including a clear-cut breakaway 4:58 into the third period that Roy stopped. Another Mogilny shot was tipped in by Sergei Brylin 4:39 into the second period.

"When Peter Forsberg went down (after round two, because of surgery to remove his spleen), they had to pick up their play," Gomez said of the adversity that confronted the Avalanche. "We talked about that and how we had to duplicate what they did, even though we hope to have Jason Arnott (injured in Game 4) back for Game 6."

Mogilny's goal was set up by a poor Colorado line switch, giving the Devils their fourth odd-man rush of the period, compared to about the same amount in the first four games of the series.

"I don't know what happened on that line switch," Tanguay said. "All I know is there was a big crowd in front of our bench while Mogilny and Gomez were playing catch out there before Mogilny scored."

To this point in the series, it was the Colorado

ALEX TANGUAY SCORED THE ONLY GOAL FOR THE AVALANCHE IN GAME 5. PATRICK ROY WAS MORE CAREFUL WHEN PLAYING THE PUCK AFTER HIS MISTAKE BEHIND THE NET COST THE TEAM GAME 4. THERE WASN'T MUCH SPACE FOR THE AVS TO MOVE AROUND IN GAME 5.

GAME 5

defense that had been hailed for stepping up into the offense and showing quick work on the transition game. But in Game 5, the Devils' defensemen played a major role in the odd-man rushes and the goals New Jersey scored. Rafalski assisted on both of the Devils' first-period goals, and Scott Niedermayer helped set up the Brylin goal.

"One of the keys to getting the defense to step up in the offense is that you can't allow yourself to be spread out in your own zone," Avalanche defenseman Adam Foote said. "When that happens to you, you have to work harder in your own zone and don't always have the energy to step up into the play."

Those long dump-ins by the Devils and strong forechecking again negated the Avalanche's talented defensive trio of Foote, Bourque and Rob Blake.

With Colorado on an important power play late in the second period, Sykora and Elias broke free once again on a 2-on-1 that was throttled when Elias fanned on his 20-footer from the right-wing faceoff circle.

The best chance the Avalanche had came just after that power play when Eric Messier was thwarted by Brodeur after a nice setup in the slot by Dan Hinote.

Meanwhile, John Madden added the final goal for the Devils with just 1:55 remaining to put New Jersey one victory away from winning its second consecutive Stanley Cup and the team's third in seven years.

"Well, I mean it's all a cliche," said Robinson, who played on six Stanley Cup championship teams when he was a member of the Montreal Canadiens. "But the last one is always the hardest one to get. I think for us the most important thing is not to look at the score, not to look at the standings, not to look at anything but each shift and play each shift like it is your last shift."

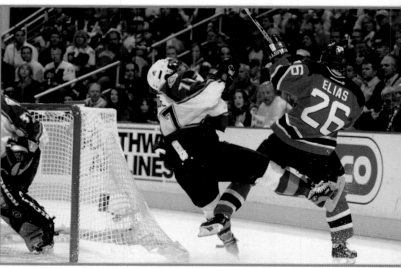

MARTIN BRODEUR MADE A HUGE SAVE ON DAVE REID EARLY IN THE GAME. SCOTT GOMEZ ASSISTED ON ALEXANDER MOGILNY'S FIRST-PERIOD GOAL. GAME 5 WAS A PHYSICAL MATCHUP AS ALEX TANGUAY GOT CRUNCHED ALONG THE BOARDS AND STEVEN REINPRECHT FOUGHT FOR ROOM WITH SERGEI NEMCHINOV. SERGEI BRYLIN DIDN'T FIND MUCH ROOM, EITHER.

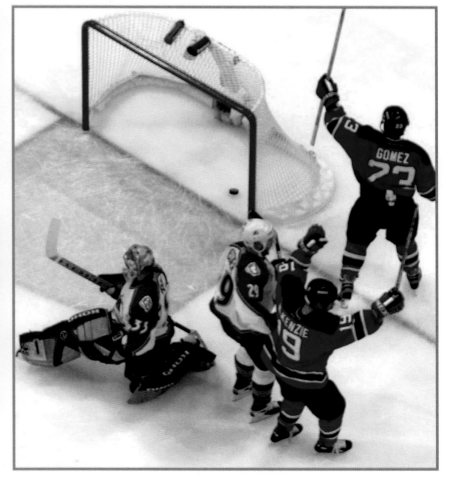

FACED AND RECORDED HIS 19TH CAREER PLAYOFF SHUTOUT.

GAME 6

June 7 at New Jersey

Avalanche	4
Devils	0

Patrick Roy came up big in Game 6. No surprise there. But how would he and the Avalanche fare in Game 7?

After seeing the Devils deny the Avs time and again in the neutral zone in Game 5, Colorado—with a big assist from Roy—returned the favor in Game 6, winning by a 4-0 score on New Jersey ice and deadlocking the Stanley Cup Finals at three games each.

"That should really make for an exciting (final game)," veteran Devils defenseman Scott Stevens said. "No one will want to fall behind because each team can put such a stranglehold on the other if they get the lead."

Colorado's win meant the Finals would have a Game 7 for the first time since 1994, when the New York Rangers edged the Vancouver Canucks. The last Game 7 before that was 1987, when the Edmonton Oilers defeated the Philadelphia Flyers for their third Stanley Cup in four years in a run that would result in five Cups in seven seasons.

In Game 6 of the 2001 Finals, the Avalanche stood tall behind Roy, who stopped all 24 shots directed his way for the 19th shutout in his playoff career, extending his NHL record. Killing off three penalties in the game's first 10 minutes was another key for Colorado.

On the minus side, though, was the reminder that Roy and the Avalanche had lost to Dallas in a pressure-packed Game 7 of the Western Conference playoffs in each of the past two seasons. Was there some kind of

GAME 6

Game 7 hex?

"I think we all got a lot of confidence from Game 7 against L.A.," Roy said of Colorado's second-round triumph this year. "Dallas isn't something that's on our minds."

Coach Bob Hartley wasn't afraid to talk about the losses to the Stars.

"Game 7s are the best learning experience you can have," he said. "Our team took both of those losses hard. But they learned they had to have a greater commitment to defense. It was the way our season ended in those two series that helped make our commitment to excellence even better this season."

With the home team having trouble holding serve in its own building during this series, you could excuse the Avs for being a bit skeptical about the advantage of playing Game 7 at Denver's Pepsi Center.

Joe Sakic, for one, had no qualms about it.

"This is something we worked hard for all year—to get Game 7 at home," Sakic said. "We're looking forward to the energy in our building. I think if we can be a little more patient like we were tonight, we can make that energy from our fans work for us."

Adam Foote, like Roy, was a major contributor in Game 6. Foote is the quintessential defenseman's defenseman, worrying only about his own zone and gladly taking on the biggest, meanest dude to start a street fight with.

In this critical game, Foote opened the scoring with a brilliant offensive move, stepping up and intercepting a dangerous cross-ice pass in the neutral zone. He made two strides into the New Jersey zone and blasted a shot past Devils goaltender Martin Brodeur for a 1-0 advantage.

THE NEW JERSEY FANS COULDN'T HELP BUT FEEL EXCITED ABOUT THE POSSIBILITY OF BACK-TO-BACK STANLEY CUPS. THE SERIES CONTINUED TO BE A ROUGH ONE. BUT AS PHYSICAL AS IT WAS, THE AVS STILL FOUND WAYS TO BEAT BRODEUR AND FORCE A GAME 7.

GAME 6

Foote later added two assists for his first three-point game since April 4, 1997. He also had three hits, two takeaways and two blocked shots. Avs defenseman Ray Bourque once named his all-warrior team, and he put Foote next to him on defense.

Thanks largely to Foote and Roy, the Avalanche kept their season alive on this night.

With the Stanley Cup in the building just in case the Devils sewed up their second straight crown, there were a few players in the New Jersey locker room who thought the Devils had blown a great opportunity to win.

"Now it's like the Super Bowl," Devils defenseman Ken Daneyko said. "One game, winner takes all. A seventh game. Isn't that what everybody in the hockey world wants? I know if you had told us back last September that we could have one game to keep our Cup, we'd have gladly taken it."

But if you had told the Devils they would lose, 4-0, at home to the Avalanche in Game 6, that same bunch would have told you they learned their lesson last year when they couldn't finish off the Dallas Stars at home in Game 5, losing 1-0 in triple overtime, before winning it all in Dallas in Game 6.

"We've done it the hard way all through the playoffs, and we'll have to do it the hard way again," Stevens said.

"When the game's over and you can't even pick one player who played well, in a huge game, believe me, it's disappointing," Devils coach Larry Robinson said. "We have to bring our work boots to Denver instead of our running shoes, the way we were running around tonight. They kicked our butts and rubbed our faces in it."

TEMPERS FLARED AS THE GAME WORE ON, WHEN BOTH TEAMS REALIZED THERE WOULD BE A GAME 7. ALTHOUGH COLORADO HAD LITTLE SPACE TO WORK WITH, PLAYERS LIKE CHRIS DRURY (BELOW) SOLVED THE DEVILS' TRAP AND EVENED THE SERIES AT THREE GAMES APIECE.

ADAM FOOTE'S FIRST GOAL OF THE FINALS PROVED TO BE THE GAME-WINNER. PATRICK ROY ROUNDED INTO FORM IN GAME 6, SHUTTING OUT NEW JERSEY AND FORCING A GAME 7. MARTIN BRODEUR COULD ONLY LOOK FORWARD TO A GAME 7 FOR HIS CHANCE AT REDEMPTION.

GAME 7

June 9 at Colorado

Avalanche	3
Devils	1

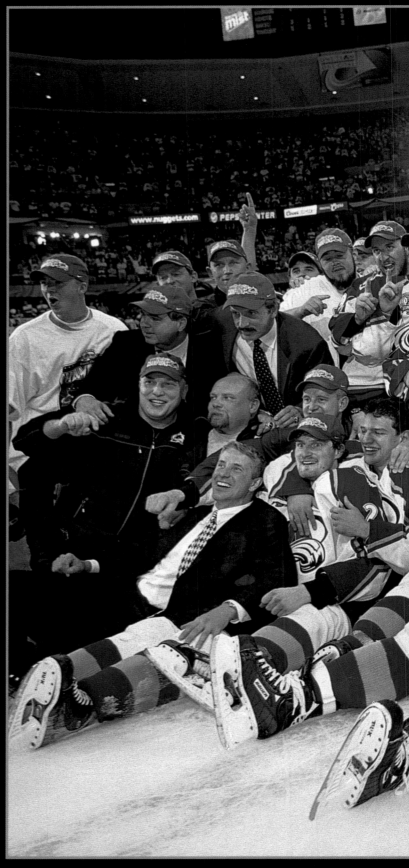

At age 40, Ray Bourque stepped onto the ice before Game 7 without a Stanley Cup to show for his 22 NHL seasons, and he perhaps wondered whether he was doomed to retire as hockey's all-time also-ran.

That's why, at game's end, Bourque skated off the ice with hockey's Holy Grail grasped tightly in his hands—and wouldn't let go.

"I remember watching John Elway from afar and rooting for him to finally win a Super Bowl — and then winning another before he retired as a champion," Bourque said.

Over his career, Bourque had skated through countless miles of frustration before the Avalanche defeated the Devils, 3-1, in Game 7 to capture the franchise's second Stanley Cup in six seasons. In terms of pure drama, it didn't get much better: Bourque's two-decade-plus quest came down to one 60-minute game on a June night in Denver.

Bourque certainly was center stage, but he wasn't the only story.

■ Patrick Roy clearly outplayed Devils goalie Martin Brodeur, who had hoped to beat his boyhood hero. Roy allowed a total of two goals in Colorado's four Finals victories.

■ Alex Tanguay, the second-year man who was benched in the Western Conference title series last year because of a lack of production, scored twice in Game 7 and tied linemate Joe Sakic for the most goals in the Finals with four.

AFTER 22 YEARS, THIS WAS THE FIRST TIME RAY BOURQUE

GAME 7

■ Sakic's speed and leadership contributed greatly to the Avalanche's resiliency. And Sakic had a goal and an assist in Game 7.

In the end, this turned out to be a punch and counterpunch series —with the team initiating the dump-ins and winning the battle in the neutral zone taking control.

Colorado scored first in the climactic game when Tanguay circled the New Jersey net and scored just 7:58 into the game. Tanguay scored again 4:57 into the second period when Devils defenseman Colin White was caught up the ice and was beaten by Adam Foote's lead pass off the glass to Sakic at center ice. Sakic was stopped by Brodeur, but Tanguay scored into an empty net on the rebound.

The Avalanche left little doubt about the game's outcome when, 79 seconds after Tanguay's second goal, Sakic beat Brodeur with a quick, screened shot through Scott Stevens' legs and high into the net.

And when it was over, Sakic, the Avalanche captain, handed the Stanley Cup to Bourque to hold it aloft in celebration. It was, to say the least, a tearful moment at the Pepsi Center.

"Win one for Ray" was the theme from the day Bourque was acquired from the Boston Bruins in March 2000. And on June 9, 2001, it came to fruition.

"I had trouble keeping it together from the national anthem on," Bourque acknowledged. "It was a very emotional night. And when it is all said and done, stories about this night are going to get better and better as we age."

"What a way to end a career," said defensive partner Rob Blake, perhaps knowing something that Bourque refused to reveal after the game.

ALEX TANGUAY HAD TWO GOALS AND AN ASSIST AND JOE SAKIC HAD A GOAL AND AN ASSIST TO PROVIDE THE OFFENSE FOR GAME 7. PATRICK ROY ALLOWED ONLY ONE GOAL OVER THE FINAL TWO GAMES TO EARN HIS THIRD CAREER CONN SMYTHE TROPHY AS MVP OF THE PLAYOFFS.

GAME 7

"It would have been a shame if Ray had left the game without a Stanley Cup," injured center Peter Forsberg said.

When the playoffs began, Bourque put on a cap that had "Mission 16W" on it—and that didn't stand for some highway exit sign on the New Jersey Turnpike. It meant 16 wins were needed from the beginning of the playoffs to hoist the Stanley Cup.

"For me, it has been a long time coming," Bourque said. "That's why I came here—to give myself an opportunity to win. It may be my last opportunity — and I was savoring every second of it."

Bourque passed on some sage advice along the way, too. A Knute Rockne-like speech it wasn't, but with his team one defeat from elimination in the Stanley Cup Finals, Bourque said he felt he had to stand up and say something to his teammates before Game 6 on the Devils' home ice.

"He talked about what a great season it had been," Sakic said. "'Why waste it with a bad effort?' He told us to look in the mirror and that we should all see a champion looking right back at us."

Bourque stepped to the middle of the locker room before Game 7 as well.

"He told us how long he had waited for this night," Foote said. "He said you can't believe how long it might take you to get back to the Finals. That broke up the room and eased the tension, knowing how long he had waited to play with the Cup on the line."

The Avalanche's 2001 championship proved that dreams do come true, even for a 40-year-old defenseman who had to play a record 1,826 National Hockey League games before finally seeing his name engraved on the Stanley Cup.

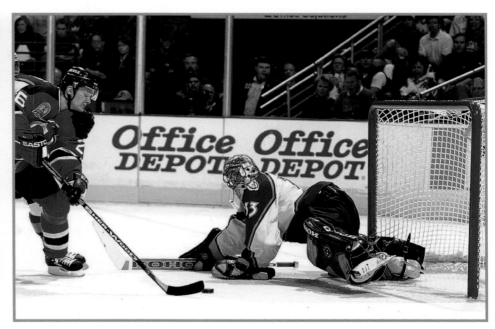

Patrick Roy came up with some huge saves on Patrik Elias and Scott Gomez, and he stopped 25 of 26 shots in Game 7. Martin Brodeur didn't fare as well, allowing three goals on 19 shots. For coach Bob Hartley, winning the Cup silenced his critics—and he had Roy, Ray Bourque and regular-season MVP Joe Sakic to thank.

There was bedlam at the Pepsi Center when the Avalanche won the Stanley Cup (held aloft by Rob Blake, above, and general manager Pierre Lacroix, opposite page) with a Game 7 victory over New Jersey. The Cup wasn't the only hardware on display—goalie Patrick Roy was awarded the Conn Smythe trophy as MVP of the NHL playoffs.

Avalanche fans and players (including Greg de Vries, immediate right, and Ray Bourque, below) could hardly contain themselves after Colorado accomplished its mission—one called "16W."

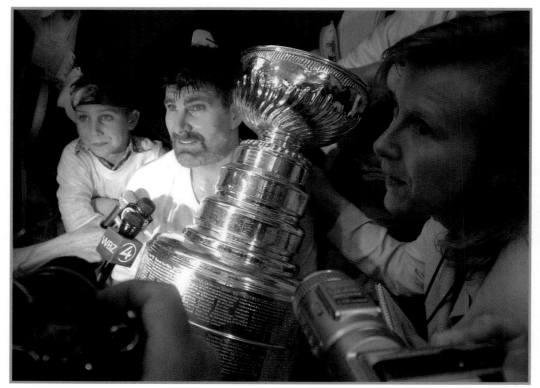

AFTER THE AVALANCHE WON ITS SECOND STANLEY CUP IN SIX SEASONS, THE TEAM GOT A ROUSING VICTORY PARADE.

Avs players were introduced one by one at the City and County Building (immediate left), where fireworks contributed to a festive occasion.

RAY BOURQUE RECEIVED A FITTING STREET SIGN FROM DENVER MAYOR WELLINGTON WEBB. MEANWHILE, PETER FORSBERG GOT AFFECTIONATE WITH THE STANLEY CUP.